Ginosko House Christmas

TOM DOLE

Ginosko House

Flowood, MS

Ginosko House Christmas
Copyright © 2019 by **Ginosko House Publishing**

All rights reserved. No part of this publication may be reproduced, distributed or transmitted in any form or by any means, without prior written permission.

Ginosko House LLC
316 Northshore Pl
Brandon MS 39047
www.ginoskohouse.com

All Scripture verses are from the New King James Version of the Holy Bible.

Cover Design © 2019 by woohoojay creative
On Instagram & Twitter at @woohoojay

Ginosko House Christmas -- 1st ed.

TABLE OF CONTENTS

Devotionals

A Note From The Author 1

One Life, One Death 6

It's Not What You Know, It's Who You Know 10

Pagan Roots?… 13

Peeking At The Gifts 17

Mary and Joseph… and Zelophehad? 22

Gimmie, Gimmie 27

House of Bread… and Love 32

The Manger 36

Willing Vessels 39

Heavenly Dynamos 42

On Giving Gifts, part 1 46

On Giving Gifts, part 2 53

What The Shepherds Saw & Heard… and Did! 57

The Beginning of Wisdom, part 1 62

The Beginning of Wisdom, part 2 66

Political Fallout 71

Prophetic Gifts – Gold 77

Prophetic Gifts – Frankincense 82

Prophetic Gifts – Myrrh 86

Celebrating Presence… not presents 91

Christmas Cheer, It's Contagious! 97

It's 'His' Star 102

Be Still and Know 106
For You! Christ is Born! Rejoice! 109
Tear Into Those Gifts! 113
The Coming King 118

Appetizers

Chicken Liver Pate' 9
Pink Shrimp Dip 12
Marinated Brussel Sprouts 16
Gazpacho 20

Desserts

Cherry Dessert 26
Christmas Wreath Punch 30
Forgotten Dessert 35
Creamy Chocolate Pie 38
French Hot Chocolate 41
Fudge Pie 45
Honey Walnut Gingerbread 49
Molasses Crinkles 51
Old Fashioned Ice Cream 55
Popcorn Balls 60

Rolling Pin Cookies 61

Semi-Sweet Nut Brittle 65

Streusel Coffee Cake 69

Entrées

Baked Stuffed-Flounder 75

Classic Roast Beef (kind of) 80

Oven Sherried Roast Beef 85

Pork Chops Over Rice 89

Bonus Entrée!

Pheasant 90

Sides & Salads

Grilled Potato Packets 95

Roasted Brussel Sprouts with Balsamic Reduction 100

Wonder Blend Salad 105

Marinated Garden Vegetables 108

Endnotes 125

Acknowledgments

Special thanks are due to the following people who in one way or another inspired, assisted, or added to the final outcome of this book:

My mother, grandmothers, aunts, and friends of the family whose recipes are found within this book, along with the memories of family gatherings surrounding those recipes.

My wife and son, Cathy and Jeremiah, who contributed a couple of recipes of their own.

My sister, Becky, who archived many of these recipes.

Jay Horne of *woohoojay creative*, who helped design and format the cover for this book. Jay can be found on Instagram and Twitter at @woohoojay.

A Note From the Author

"It's the most wonderful time of the year…"

IT'S ONE LINE FROM A POPULAR CHRISTMAS SONG, and I heartily agree with its sentiment. In fact, from sometime around the middle of November to the end of Christmas is, to me, the most wonderful time of the year. The song goes on to describe "kids jingle belling", marshmallow toasting (we never did this at Christmas) and ghost stories (the only ghost story that goes with Christmas is Charles Dicken's *A Christmas Carol*), mistletoeing, good cheer, caroling, snow, parties, and holiday greetings. All of which has nothing to do with the real Christmas.

Oh, please don't misunderstand. The celebrations, the good cheer, the snow and sledding, caroling and cards, and all the gatherings with family and friends, even the shopping trips, are all wonderful, they are a part of the season. But they are all temporal. They appeal to our soul and will only make us feel happy for a while. When it comes to Christmas there is a deeper, longer-lasting element. It feeds more than the soul; it feeds the spirit. That element is, of course, Jesus Christ, the One on whom the entire story of Christmas is centered.

Without the Heart of Christmas, all those temporary delights quickly become bland and dry. We won't be able to cheer ourselves up, let alone cheer up those around us. But, with the Heart of Christmas beating in us, we can lift up those around us who don't have family or friends to do just that. These are two sides of Christmas. The temporal side with which we consume life, and the Beating Heart of Christmas with which we give life.

One Christmas season my Dad grew tired of the commercialism and overdone attempts to offer the true meaning of Christmas through consuming products and entertainment. So, he re-wrote the lyrics to "Hark The Harold Angels Sing" as follows:

Hark the herald angels sing,
Buy your gifts at Silverstein's.
Peace on earth and mercy mild,
We got toys for every child.

Rocks and books and all your bling,
We got even diamond rings.
Hark the herald angels sing,
Buy your gifts at Silverstein's.

It was his wry attempt at keeping our focus on the real Christmas. Another person put it this way:[1]

If I decorate my house perfectly with plaid bows, strands of twinkling lights and shiny balls, but do not show love to my family, I'm just another decorator.

If I slave away in the kitchen, baking dozens of Christmas cookies, preparing gourmet meals and arranging a beautifully adorned table at mealtime, but do not show love to my family, I'm just another cook.

If I work at the soup kitchen, carol in the nursing home and give all that I have to charity, but do not show love to my family, it profits me nothing.

If I trim the spruce with shimmering angels and crocheted snowflakes, attend a myriad of holiday parties and sing in the choir's cantata but do not focus on Christ, I have missed the point.

Love stops the cooking to hug the child.

Love sets aside the decorating to kiss the husband.

Love is kind, even though harried and tired.

Love doesn't envy another's home that has coordinated Christmas china and table linens.

Love doesn't yell at the kids to get out of the way, but is thankful they are there to be in the way.

Love doesn't give only to those who are able to give in return, but rejoices in giving to those who can't. Video games will break, pearl necklaces will be lost, golf clubs will rust, but giving the gift of love will endure.

Love bears all things, believes all things, hopes all things, endures all things.

Love never fails.

In a nutshell, that's the two sides of Christmas. We can feed our souls and try to please ourselves with all the temporal delights of the season. And if that is all we feed on at Christmas, it will be a shallow season at best. We'll get fed up with hearing the same songs over and over, with the crowds, with yet another party, and on and on. We'll be glad when it's all over.

But, if we feed our spirit with the true meaning of Christmas, it will surely warm our hearts with a breath of life that we can extend to family, friends, and strangers all year long, a breath of life that lingers all year long until the next Christmas season rolls around.

And so this cookbook, filled with what I hope are a few recipes you will find useful during the Christmas season. A few recipes that will add some good cheer to the gatherings of your family and friends.

But, also some food for your spirit. Some food that will breathe a breath of fresh long-lasting life into you. A truly life-changing breath of life that comes from the One who originated the whole Christmas celebration! This is most likely what Jesus meant when He said, *Man shall not live by bread alone, but by every Word that proceeds from the mouth of God.*'[2] So go ahead, enjoy the food, the gatherings, the caroling, and all the other things. They are part of the celebration. Just don't leave out the Beating Heart of Christmas.

About The Recipes

With the exception of a couple of recipes from my wife and son, most of these recipes range in age from thirty to seventy years old (yup!). They come from my parents and grandparents and their friends. Some of them used ingredients such as sugar, (lots of it), and shortening. Since these ingredients are no longer popular, please feel free to substitute (or not). There are enough entrée's, sides & salads, and appetizers for one complete meal every week of December. There are enough desserts to make one every other day from December 2 to 26 (hey, it's Christmas!)

The recipes for the daily devotionals… Oh, they're much older. You see, they are from the Ancient of Days. As much as your grandparents, parents, family, and friends love you, He loves you more. He loves you with a great, forever love which began before He ever created heaven and earth. And He has been pursuing you with that forever love since before the beginning of time.

You may rightly ask, why are there no "template" prayers at the end of each devotional. Well, for just that reason, they would be "template" prayers. They would be someone else's prayers, my prayers, not your prayers. As you read each day's devotional, my open and heartfelt prayer is that you will develop your own personal relationship with the Living God – Jesus Christ. That you begin to know Him through the devotionals so you can talk with Him yourself. Why use my prayers, or someone else's prayers, that are based on our relationship with God, but not your relationship. *You* get to know Him. That's why we celebrate Christmas.

Christmas truly is the most wonderful time of the year! So, from myself and from Ginosko House, to your family and your house…

~ *Merry Christmas!* ~

…underneath all the bulging bundles is this beating heart of Christmas."

~George Matthew Adam

One Life, One Death
December 1

IT IS ONE OF THE MOST COMMON MESSAGES heard at Christmastime:

> *For unto us a Child is born, unto us a Son is given;*
> *and the government will be upon His shoulder,*
> *and His name will be called*
> *Wonderful, Counselor,*
> *Mighty God,*
> *Everlasting Father,*
> *Prince of Peace.* [1]

At Christmas this verse is seen on posters and Christmas cards, it's heard in songs, and it's even used in advertisements. But just who is the "Child" that was "born unto us"? Who is the "Son" that was "given unto us"?

Notice the difference in the phrases: "a Child is born", "a Son is given". Each phrase is referring to a different event. Isaiah 9:6 is prophetic. The fulfillment of the first phrase, *"unto us a Child is born"*, occurred on a night long ago in 2 B.C., in a small town named Bethlehem. On that night, which we now celebrate as Christmas, a young baby was born. That baby was human. On that night in Bethlehem, a Child was *"born unto us",* so that we might be born-again as children of God.

> *But you, Bethlehem Ephrathah,*
> *though you are little among the thousands of Judah,*
> *yet out of you shall come forth to Me*
> *the One to be Ruler in Israel,*
> *whose goings forth are from of old, from everlasting.*[2]

*Then the angel said to them,
'Do not be afraid, for behold,
I bring you good tidings of great joy which will be to all people.
For there is born to you this day in the city of David a Savior,
who is Christ the Lord.
And this will be the sign to you:
You will find a Babe wrapped in swaddling cloths,
lying in a manger."* [3]

The fulfillment of the second prophetic phrase, *"unto us a Son is given"*, was fulfilled on a hill called Golgotha thirty-three years later. The Son that was *"given"* on the Cross that day was divine! That sacrifice of God's only Son on the Cross was the fulfillment of a prophecy given by Abraham at the Akedah, the enactment of Abraham sacrificing his only son, Isaac. [4] As Abraham prepares for the sacrifice, Isaac asks, *"Look, the fire and the wood, but where is the lamb for a burnt offering?"* Abraham replies, *"My son, God will provide <u>Himself</u> the lamb for a burnt offering."*[5]

God interrupted the proceedings before Abraham strikes Isaac. But the true sacrifice is finished two thousand years later at the very same location when another Father gives His Son as the sacrifice for our sins. God <u>Himself</u> became the Lamb that was sacrificed.

It was the act of ultimate love, reiterated in John 3:16, *For God so loved the world that He gave His only begotten Son..."* God so loved, He gave. That's the essence of Christmas... *not getting, but giving.* The world today has it backwards! Isaiah 9:6 unwraps God's gift to us a little further:

*His name is
Wonderful, Counselor,
Mighty God, Everlasting Father,
Prince of Peace.*

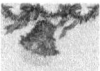 We will keep "unwrapping" God's gift over the next few days, right up to Christmas Day. In the meantime…

~ *Merry Christmas!* ~

*"I sometimes think we expect too much of Christmas Day.
We try to crowd into it the long arrears
of kindliness and humanity of the whole year.
As for me, I like to take my Christmas a little at a time,
all through the year.
And thus I drift along into the holidays –
waking up some fine morning and suddenly saying to myself,
'Why, this is Christmas Day!"*

~ David Grayson

APPETIZER

Chicken Liver Pate'

INGREDIENTS

1 lb. Chicken livers   2 Tbs. butter
1½ tsp salt   1 tsp. mixed herbs
2 eggs hard-cooked, chopped

PREPARATION

1. Simmer chicken livers in salted water until tender.
2. Drain water from livers, chop, and add eggs.
3. Sauté' onions in butter.
4. Chop or blend all ingredients to a fine paste.

It's Not What You Know, It's Who You Know

December 2

WHY DO WE CELEBRATE JESUS' BIRTHDAY, Christmas, on December 25th?

History is a study of cause and effect; it connects events through time. No one else in history has impacted individuals, families, cultures, or nations more than Jesus Christ. His birth is undeniable. Yet, the date of his birth is lost to history. The Bible leaves the actual date unknown. Well, almost unknown. Taking part in the treasure hunt does yield rewards.

There are clues in Scripture as to when His birth may have occurred. First of all, we are told the shepherds were in the fields watching their sheep.[1] In Israel, late Fall and Winter is a time for sheep to be in protected areas, not out in open fields. This would imply a date prior to October.

Also, there was a census being conducted by Rome. Surely, Caesar Augustus and his administrators were wise enough to know that requiring people to travel during winter, when the weather and road conditions were awful, would result in poor census data (and thus lower tax revenues).

Another piece of evidence can be found in the birth of John the Baptist, whose Dad and Mom were Zacharias and Elizabeth.

Zacharias was a priest serving in the Temple at Jerusalem during the course of Abijah.[2] Historically the course of Abijah is known to be from June 13-19 of that year. It was during this Temple service that Zacharias was prophetically told that he and Elizabeth would have a son.[3] Presumably, when Zacharias returned home after his Temple service was over, is the time when John the Baptist was conceived by Elizabeth.

When Jesus was conceived by Mary, Elizabeth was already six months pregnant.[4] So, when Mary went to visit Elizabeth, it would have been six months after June, sometime in December. This means John would have been born sometime in March of the following year.

Therefore, Jesus would have been born six months after John, giving His birth a September time frame. Based on Israel's feast days some scholars pinpoint Jesus' date of birth as September 29th.

While this is all thought-provoking information, why is it that the actual birth date of Jesus remains unknown? It turns out that it is not the date that is important. It is the person whose birth we celebrate that is important. Jesus Himself, put it this way: *"Eternal life is knowing God, and Jesus Christ..."*,[5] not knowing "about" Him. What do you know, it's true: It's not what you know, it's Who you know!

Who is He really?
Why was He born?
What is the proper way to celebrate His birth?

"And you shall have joy and exultant delight, and many will rejoice over His birth."[6]

~ *Merry Christmas!* ~

"The Church does not superstitiously observe days, merely as days, but as memorials of important facts. Christmas might be kept as well upon one day of the year as another; but there should be a stated day for commemorating the birthday of our Savior, because there is danger that what may be done on any day, will be neglected."

~ Samuel Johnson

APPETIZER

Pink Shrimp Dip

INGREDIENTS

6 Tbs. chili sauce	1 tsp. onion juice
4 Tbs. lemon juice	½ tsp. Worchester sauce
2/3 cup milk	2 cups creamy cottage cheese
1 lb. shrimp, freshly cleaned and cooked	

PREPARATION

1. Finely chop shrimp and add cottage cheese.

2. Stir in chili sauce, onion juice, lemon juice, and Worchester sauce; gradually beat in enough milk to give dipping consistency.

3. Serve with fresh vegetable dunking-sized food: celery, carrots, cauliflower, etc.

Pagan Roots?

December 3

IF JESUS BIRTHDAY IS NOT ON DECEMBER 25TH, how did that come to be the day we celebrate as His birthday?

You remember Nimrod, the guy in the Bible who tried to build a tower that reached to the heavens? It seems he had a son named Tammuz, who was married to a gal named Semiramis. As the story goes, Tammuz was linked with the Babylonian Sun God. When the Winter Solstice approached, around December 22nd or 23rd, the days grew shorter, and there was less daylight. Pagan worshippers grew concerned that the light might never return (gasp!). Tammuz, who was called the "the dying god", supposedly died on the day of the winter solstice.

But, the following morning the rebirth of Tammuz would be celebrated. After the solstice, when the days began to lengthen and daylight grew longer, mighty festivals were held celebrating the return of the sun, and looking toward the coming of Spring. A tree would be brought into the house and decorated. The fireplace would be filled with logs representing the re-birth of Tammuz. They were called "yule" logs. Yule is the ancient Babylonian word for "child". People would feast as long as the logs burned.

All occult rituals have their roots in ancient Babylonian pagan worship. Other pagan occultists have similar solstice rituals. As empires rose and fell, the pagan rituals that remained were carried from one power center to another. In the month of December, ancient Iranians worshipped the mystery god Mithra. Other gods who were worshipped around the time of the winter solstice included Baal, Horus, Osiris, Dionysus, Hercules, Perseus, and, Helios.

The power center for occult worship eventually moved to Rome. They used the same gods but gave them different names.

The Romans worshipped the god Saturn with a seven-day festival beginning December 17th. Festivities included giving gifts, decorating homes with evergreen boughs, and raucous merry-making.

In A.D. 313 Emperor Constantine issued his Edict of Toleration. The changes that followed, allowed the pagan rituals of the winter solstice to be covered with a "Christian" veneer. In 440 A.D., when Christian fathers officially adopted the date of December 25th as the celebration of Christ's birth, it was merely a leftover of the occult traditions which had been carried down through the years from the pagan rituals of ancient Babylon.

So, what does any of this have to do with the birth of Jesus and the celebration Christians call Christmas?

Nothing.

Is the Christian celebration on December 25th involved in paganism? Absolutely not!

Why not, you may ask?

Because God began His preparations for the arrival of Jesus on the earth long before He even created heaven and earth.

The prophecies concerning Jesus first arrival on earth were written down long before the actual events ever happened. The very fact that those prophecies were declared and written well in advance of the historical events proves the eternal nature of God. He dwells outside our time domain in the realm of eternity. And that is why He is able to know what will happen before it happens. God's prophetic utterances in the Bible are His way of letting us know what His plans are.

So, is it okay to celebrate Christmas on December 25th? Yes, it is; as long as the celebrations are not occultic, but fitting for the King of kings. Romans 14 makes it clear we are not to let others judge the way we celebrate a day, as long as we observe the day as unto the Lord.

The true message of Christmas as found in the Bible is the authoritative and verifiable story of God's great love for mankind, and the lengths He went to in rescuing and paying the ransom for His Beloved. So, our question now becomes, what is the message of Christmas?

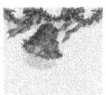

~ *Merry Christmas!* ~

*"Christmas is the time for kindling
the fire of hospitality in the hall,
the genial flame of charity in the heart."*

~ Washington Irving

APPETIZER

Marinated Brussel Sprouts

INGREDIENTS

2 - 10 oz. pkgs. frozen Brussel sprouts

1 small clove garlic, minced

1 Tbs. onion, finely chopped

1 tsp. parsley, dried flakes

½ tsp. dried dillweed (can use dill seed)

½ cup Italian salad dressing, low-cal (or not)

PREPARATION

1. Cook Brussel sprouts according to directions on package; drain and cool.
2. Combine all other ingredients and pour over Brussel sprouts.
3. Marinate in refrigerator for several hours.
4. Drain and serve with cocktail picks.

Peeking At The Gifts

December 4

IF WE DO NOT WANT TO CELEBRATE CHRISTMAS as a pagan holiday, what do we need to know about its real meaning?

We can all remember, as children, the eager anticipation of waiting for Christmas morning so we could open gifts. We knew the gifts would be waiting for us, but we didn't know what they were because there was no peeking ahead of time, (or at least there shouldn't have been any peeking!) Our parents had carefully preserved the secrets of the gifts.

The birth of Christ, which we now celebrate as Christmas, was an event which was also eagerly anticipated... by God. In fact, God so eagerly anticipated the restoration of His fellowship with us that He couldn't wait, but had to tell us ahead of time what He was doing for us, and what He was preparing for us. He let us peek at the gifts He had prepared for us!

Yes, God told us in advance about the gifts He had waiting for us on the first Christmas Day. And, He told us what would be the benefit of those gifts for years to come. God told us ahead of time what city the Christ would be born in:

But you, Bethlehem Ephrathah,
though you are little among the thousands of Judah,
yet out of you shall come forth to Me the One to be Ruler in Israel,
whose goings forth are from of old, from everlasting.[1]

God told us ahead of time what His mission for the Christ would be:

*Indeed He says,
'It is too small a thing that You should be My Servant
to raise up the tribes of Jacob,
and to restore the preserved ones of Israel;
I will also give You as a light to the Gentiles,
that You should be My salvation to the ends of the earth.* [2]

God told us ahead of time that the Christ would be born of a virgin:

*Therefore the Lord Himself will give you a sign:
Behold, the virgin shall conceive and bear a Son,
and shall call His name Immanuel.* [3]

God told us ahead of time that the Christ was destined to sit upon the throne of David and to rule and reign forever:

*Behold, you will conceive in your womb and bring forth a Son,
and shall call His name Jesus.
He will be great, and will be called the Son of the Highest;
and the Lord God will give Him the throne of His father David.
And He will reign over the house of Jacob forever,
and of His kingdom there will be no end.* [4]

Oh! God was excited!

Now, consider this question: When did God start making arrangements for your care and well-being, when did God start making arrangements for your salvation?

He chose us in Him before the foundation of the world...in love... [5]

The story of Christmas began in the heart of God long before He created heaven and earth. God had you in mind before He created anything. Knowing ahead of time the decisions and actions Adam and Eve would make, a loving Heavenly Father began making preparations to pay the ransom required for our rescue. And, He made those preparations first before He did anything else.

Many people make the claim that they have "found God". But it is not we who went looking for God; we were the ones who were lost, it is God who went looking for us.

You did not choose Me, but I chose you... [6]

God from the beginning chose you for salvation... [7]

Not only was God thinking about us far in advance, but He also told us - in advance - about all the preparations he was making in order to buy us back. All these things that God told us in advance we call prophecy. Scripture says God is *"the High and Lofty One, Who inhabits eternity..."*[8] From His position in eternity God can see the end of all things and the beginning of all things. This gives Him the unique ability to declare those things which have not yet happened, but which will happen according to His plans.

The full fruition of His plans for you began to unfold on a star-lit night in Judea two thousand years ago...

~ *Merry Christmas!* ~

"Christmas is not just a time for festivity and merry-making.
It is more than that.
It is a time for the contemplation of eternal things.
The Christmas spirit is a spirit of giving and forgiving."

~ J. C. Penny

APPETIZER

Gazpacho

INGREDIENTS

1 Pint cherry Tomatoes
2 Garlic cloves, minced
1 tsp Worcestershire sauce
¼ tsp dried Herbes De Provence
1 Tbsp aged balsamic vinegar

1 Lime, juiced
½ tsp ground cumin
¼ Cup olive oil
¼ tsp cayenne pepper
1 tsp kosher salt

1 Small bunch of cilantro, ¼ cup finely chopped
4 Tomatoes, large, peeled and diced
1 Cucumber, medium, peeled and diced
1 Red bell pepper, diced (approx. ½ cup)
Freshly ground pepper to taste

GINOSKO HOUSE CHRISTMAS

PREPARATION

1. Combine diced tomatoes, cucumber, bell pepper, cilantro and garlic into a large bowl.

2. Stir in salt, cumin, Herbes De Provence, cayenne pepper, and black pepper.

3. Place cherry tomatoes, olive oil, lime juice, balsamic vinegar, and Worcestershire sauce in a blender. Puree until smooth.

4. Pour pureed mixture through a strainer into the tomato-cucumber mixture.

5. Stir to combine then return all ingredients in the bowl into a blender (in batches if you prefer). Puree until smooth or to your desired consistency.

6. Refrigerate the mixture until thoroughly chilled, about 2-3 hours.

7. Taste the soup for salt and pepper before serving. Ladle into small bowls or chilled cups and garnish with cilantro ribbons. Alternatively: you can also top this soup with chilled steamed lobster, crab or shrimp!

Serves 4 to 6.

Mary and Joseph… and Zelophehad?

December 5

JOSEPH AND MARY WERE THE EARTHLY PARENTS of Jesus. While much (often too much) is made of Mary, very little is mentioned concerning Joseph. Yet both are extremely important in the Christmas story.

It seems there were a couple of small problems caused a few centuries before the inn became full, or shepherds saw a marvelous sight, or before a baby was wrapped in swaddling clothes and laid in a manger.

Back in the days of Moses, there was a fellow named Zelophehad. The time had come for Israel to enter in and take possession of the Promised Land. Zelophehad had been blessed with daughters, but no sons. In short, he had no sons who would be able to lay claim to any land, and thus, his daughters would be left without an inheritance.

Yet Zelophehad's daughters were persistent. They petitioned Moses for an inheritance. Moses, in turn, petitioned the Lord on their behalf. The girls were given an exception to the "rules of inheritance." The exception said, "if a man has no sons his daughters may receive his inheritance *if they marry within their tribe*." When the daughter marries within her own tribe, the bride's father *legally adopts her husband as his son* thus, providing the daughters with an inheritance.

Now, let's fast forward a few hundred years to the time of Jeconiah, a descendant of King David. Remember that God had promised David that his descendant would sit on the throne in Jerusalem:

> *He shall build a house for My name,*
> *and I will establish the throne of his kingdom forever.* [1]

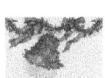

He will be great,
and will be called the Son of the Highest;
and the Lord God will give Him the throne of His father David.
And He will reign over the house of Jacob forever,
and of His kingdom there will be no end. [2]

Jeconiah was one in a long line of "bad egg" kings who consistently ignored God's covenants, resisted the counsel of His will, and promoted "the Lie". Jeconiah purposely led Israel into idolatry. Having had enough of idolatrous kings leading His nation astray, God placed a blood curse on Jeconiah and all of his descendants.

Thus says the LORD:
'Write this man down as childless,
a man who shall not prosper in his days;
for none of his descendants shall prosper,
sitting on the throne of David, and ruling anymore in Judah. [3]

Had God forgotten His promise to David? This would all seem to pose a rather serious problem, a "fly in the ointment" of the Christmas story. You can almost see the gleam in Satan's eye as he begins to think his evil plans might be working. Now, there is a blood curse on the royal line. And, God put it there! If Jeconiah and his descendants are cut off, how could God keep His promise to David? How could Jesus, a descendant of David, sit on the throne?

Praise God for His mercy and wisdom ...and for Zelophehad's little girls! Recall the exception to the rules of inheritance God granted those girls: when the daughter marries within her own tribe, the bride's father legally adopts her husband as his son thus, providing the daughters with an inheritance. It is this exception to the rules of inheritance that we find working for Jesus. This exception to the rules of inheritance anticipated the blood curse placed on Jeconiah, and thus, on the lineage of Jesus.

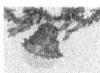

Matthew's genealogy traces Jesus' legal right to the royal throne through Jeconiah to Joseph, Mary's husband. This makes Jesus the legal heir to the royal line, but not by blood due to the blood curse placed on Jeconiah.

Luke's genealogy traces Jesus' bloodline to the royal throne through David. Then, instead of tracing the line through Jeconiah, Luke traces it through Nathan to Heli, Mary's father. As it turns out, Heli had no sons. So, when Mary wed Joseph, Heli adopted Joseph as his son. Since Heli's lineage did not include Jeconiah, a blood right to the throne is established for Jesus.

Jesus is of the house and lineage of David through two different lines. Matthew's genealogy establishes Jesus' legal right to the royal throne through Joseph, but not the blood right due to the blood curse placed on Jeconiah. Luke's genealogy establishes His blood right to the throne through Heli and Mary.

God dwells in eternity. He is not time-limited. God

declares the end from the beginning,
and from ancient times things that are not yet done,
saying, 'My counsel shall stand, and I will do all My pleasure. [4]

God cared enough about the daughters of Zelophehad to make an exception to His own laws in order to provide for their well-being. As God made that exception, He saw, in advance the day when He would place a blood curse on Jeconiah and the line of David. God personally arranged all these events, foreseeing a Baby lying in a manger who would grow to become a man. God saw that man being nailed to a cross, giving His life in place of your life. God also sees that same man raised from the dead and seated on the Throne of David.

All this gives a whole new insight into Romans 8:38-39, doesn't it? God knows the number of hairs on our head; He knows what happens to every sparrow. He cares for the individual. He takes care of every detail of His plan for our redemption. He knows how to handle man's sinfulness without breaking His Word or failing in His purposes.

The Christmas Story and its true meaning begins to take shape...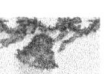

~ Merry Christmas! ~

*"Let us remember that the Christmas heart is a giving heart,
a wide-open heart that thinks of others first.
The birth of the baby Jesus stands
as the most significant event in all history,
because it has meant the pouring into a sick world
the healing medicine of love
which has transformed all manner of hearts
for almost two thousand years.
Underneath all the bulging bundles
is this beating heart of Christmas."*

~ George Matthes Adams

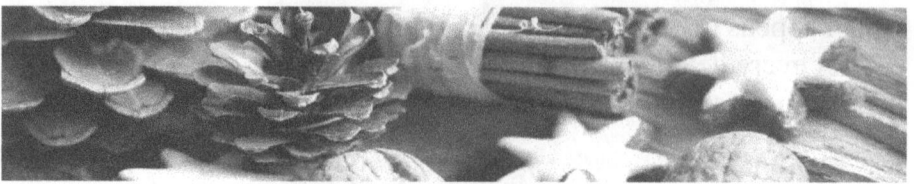

DESSERT

Cherry Dessert

INGREDIENTS

- 1 cup oatmeal
- 1 cup butter
- 1 #2 can sour cherries
- 1\3 cup sugar
- 1 cup brown sugar
- 1 cup flour.
- 4 Tbs. Tapioca, quick mix

PREPARATION

1. Combine oatmeal, brown sugar, butter, and flour as for a pie crust, put into an 8"x12" pan; save some of the mixture for the top.
2. Drain cherries and save the juice.
3. To the juice add the tapioca and sugar.
4. Cook over low heat stirring constantly, until thick.
5. Add cherries, and cool slightly.
6. Pour over unbaked crust and sprinkle remaining crumbs on top.
7. Bake 30 minutes at 350°F.

Gimmie, Gimmie

December 6

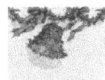

THE GIMMIE, THE GETTING, THE PUSHING, the shoving, the lines, the stress, the weariness, one more name crossed off the gift list. Oops, one more added. Surely, we'll be glad when Christmas is over!

Songs and stories of flying reindeer, fat men in red suits, and snowmen, and Grinch's, and holly, and magic trains; over and over and over and over... surely we'll be glad when Christmas is done!

Many, many years ago, there was a man – yes, a real man - named Nicholas. He wasn't a "saint" in the canonical sense, but he was a Christian. It is an interesting thing about the heart of a Christian - *freely it has received, freely it gives.*[1] The "gimmie-gimmie" in the hearts of true Christians diminishes with each passing day.

Nicholas lived in Turkey around 300 AD. His parents taught him devotion to God and generosity to the poor. His parents died when he was a teenager, but their lessons in godliness stayed with him. Nicholas eventually became the bishop of a church in a small village. His diligence in studying the Word of God and in prayer, as well as his good works, were well known among the people. One report mentions twin brothers being raised from the dead as a result of Nicholas' prayers.

Another report particularly mentions his generosity to a poor man who had three daughters. The man was so poor he had no dowry for his oldest daughter, so he was preparing to sell her into "white slavery". To help the man avoid this disgrace Nicholas threw a bag of gold coins through his window one night. Now the eldest daughter could avoid shame and be married.

St. Nicholas gave his gifts secretly because he wanted God to

get the credit. Does God get the credit in the gifts *we* give? Do the gifts *we* give reveal something of our love, of God's love?

God's giving began in Genesis 3:15 with His promise to provide a Savior through the Seed of the woman. He's been giving ever since. But then, God is love, and that is what love does; it gives.

When the time came for the second daughter to be married, Nicholas did the same thing. And again, when the time came for the third daughter to be married. But this time the girl's father caught him. Nicholas extracted a promise from the man to never tell what happened as long as Nicholas was alive.

Nicholas died on December 6, 343 AD. His remains were moved from Turkey to Bari, Italy in 1087. Stories of his life were already known, but it was now that those stories began to spread. December 6th became known as St. Nicholas Day and became a customary day of gift-giving in France and Europe. But, over time folklore and fables began to distort the true nature and character of Nicholas' gift-giving.

In Holland and Belgium, it was "Sinter Klause", and in Germany, it was "Nicholas robed in fur", both of whom gave gifts to good children and switches to bad children. As these various stories immigrated to America, they blended into one figure. By the end of the Civil War the man once known as Nicholas, who was known for his Christian charity, was now called Santa Claus.

The flying reindeer, red suit, the big belly, the pack of toys, elves at the North Pole, and the other fables were added through poems, stories, and advertising gimmicks. The folklore slowly eroded away the truth of Nicholas' life. The advertising... well, you know what that's for… and you know where the gimmie and the stress come from. The lifelong testimony of a man who demonstrated the giving heart of God was slowly mutated into an advertising gimmick to boost profits. So, it is with the world. God doesn't give switches and coal,

He only gives good gifts;[2], in fact, He loads every day with His benefits.[3]

There is one gift, which, when it is received at Christmas or any other time, is the greatest gift of all. "Christmas" is a compound word. "Christ" means "anointing", and "mass" means "celebration". Christmas is the celebration of the birth of the One whose anointing would break off the yoke of our bondage.

God so loved...that He gave... [4] The root cause of God's giving is love. What is the root cause of our giving? If it is because *"...freely we have received, freely give"*, it will bring a joy and warmth and peace to our families and to our Christmas we could never have dreamed of. Then we'll never want Christmas to end... and it won't!

Thanks be to God for His indescribable gift! [5]

~ *Merry Christmas!* ~

"When we ask our children
'What do you want for Christmas?',
we are asking a question that breeds selfishness.
In order to develop selflessness,
we should be asking
'What are you going to give?'
Christmas is the celebration of God's great gift-giving...
'For God so loved the world that he gave...'"

~ Robert Flatt

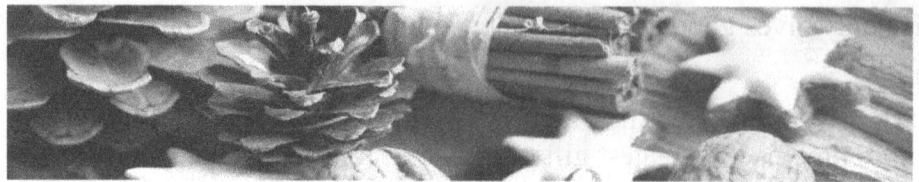

Punch

Christmas Wreath Punch

> *INGREDIENTS*
>
> 13 Red maraschino cherries, drained
>
> 13 Green maraschino cherries, drained
>
> 2 - #2 cans grapefruit juice, unsweetened
>
> 2 cans Limeade, frozen concentrate
>
> 2 - #2 cans pineapple juice
>
> 3 - 1 qt. bottles Ginger ale
>
> 1 qt. water
>
> 3 qts. ice, chopped
>
> ½ cup boiling water

GINOSKO HOUSE CHRISTMAS

TO MAKE WREATH
(may be made one day before using)

1. Wash excess color from cherries.

2. Arrange alternated colors of cherries in the bottom of a 1¼ quart ring mold.

3. Pour on enough boiling water to cover cherries.

4. Fill mold to the top with cold boiled water, freeze solid.

TO MAKE PUNCH

1. In a punch bowl, blend undiluted limeade, lemonade, pineapple, and grapefruit juice.

2. Just before serving, stir in ginger ale, 1 quart water, and ice.

3. Unmold wreath on top of punch, first setting mold briefly in a little hot water. Makes about 50 punch cup servings.

House of Bread... and Love
December 7

*"O, little town of Bethlehem,
How still we see thee lie,
Above the deep and dreamless streets,
The silent stars go by.
Yet in thy dark streets shineth,
The everlasting Light..."*

THE NAME BETHLEHEM MEANS "HOUSE OF BREAD". Thus, it is fitting that the One called "the Bread of Life" should have been born in Bethlehem. Bethlehem has a long history. And as it turns out, it is a history that demonstrates real love.

Bethlehem is located only 5½ miles south-southwest of Jerusalem on a road known as the "way of the Patriarchs". During the time of Jesus' birth, the land surrounding Bethlehem was good for growing olive groves, grapes, almonds, and figs.[1] Even though Bethlehem is *"little among the thousands of Judah"*, it is now one of the most well-known towns in Israel. Primarily because of the events that took place there one special night, events that were foretold far in advance.

Jacob, of Old Testament fame, is listed in the New Testament's "Hall of Faith" in Hebrews chapter 11. Jacob, the guy who lied and stole his brother's birthright, is listed for our example in the Bible as a "man of faith". Jacob was the man who met God face-to-face and wrestled with Him. Jacob named the place where the wrestling match took place *Peniel,* which means "face of God". Jacob's words were, *For I have seen God face to face, and my life is preserved.*[2]

As a result of his wrestling match with God, Jacob received a new name, Israel, and a new destiny. No longer would he be called

Jacob, meaning *"supplanter"*, but he would be called Israel, meaning "a prince who prevails with God." In Jacob's time, Bethlehem was known as Ephrath, which means "fruitful". It was the burial place of Rachel, Jacob's wife, and is still revered by Israelis as a sacred shrine.

Bethlehem was also the setting for the Book of Ruth, where the romance of Boaz and Ruth took place. The story that takes place in the Book of Ruth is one of the greatest stories of romance and love in literature. It is a story which proclaims that what the Law cannot do, God's grace can.

The Book of Ruth tells more than the story of the love between Boaz and Ruth. It is the story of God's love for mankind. It is the story of the Kinsman-Redeemer who assumes all the obligations of the one He loves and pays the price to reveal His love for, and to gain the love of, His redeemed. That story of love and redemption was realized on a quiet night in Bethlehem... centuries after the story of Ruth and Boaz.

Ruth had a great-grandson, David, by name. David was a boy who lived in Bethlehem tending his father's sheep, until the day Samuel showed up and anointed him king over Israel. It was after David actually became king of Israel that Bethlehem came to be called "the City of David".

And, it was to Bethlehem that Joseph and Mary returned, to take part in the census ordered by Caesar Augustus. While they were there Mary gave birth in a stable where livestock was kept. Thus, Bethlehem became the birthplace of the Messiah just as God prophesied centuries before:

But you, Bethlehem Ephrathah,
though you are little among the thousands of Judah,
yet out of you shall come forth to Me the One to be Ruler in Israel,
whose goings forth are from of old,
from everlasting. [3]

Once again, when did God begin His plans for you?
Before He ever created heaven or earth.

~ *A Christmas Proclamation!* ~

*"The spirit of Christmas needs to be superseded
by the Spirit of Christ.
The spirit of Christmas is annual;
the Spirit of Christ is eternal.
The spirit of Christmas is sentimental;
the Spirit of Christ is supernatural.
The spirit of Christmas is a human product;
the Spirit of Christ is a divine person.
That makes all the difference in the world!"*

~ Stuart Briscoe

GINOSKO HOUSE CHRISTMAS

DESSERT

Forgotten Dessert

INGREDIENTS

5 egg whites	¼ tsp. salt
½ tsp. cream of tartar	1 ½ cups sugar
1 tsp. vanilla	½ pint cream

PREPARATION

1. Preheat oven to 450°F.

2. Beat egg whites until fairly stiff, then add sugar 1 Tbs. at a time, beating until very stiff.

3. Add 1 tsp. vanilla.

4. Place into 8" x 13" greased pan.

5. Place pan in oven, turn oven off; retire for the night.

6. In the morning, add ½ pint of cream and spread over top; place in ice box until serving time.

7. Spread with fruit, fresh or canned. Cut in squares and serve.

The Manger
December 8

"Away in a manger, no crib for a bed;
The little Lord Jesus lay down His sweet head.
The stars in the sky looked down where He lay,
The little Lord Jesus asleep in the hay."

JUSTIN MARTYR, ONE OF THE EARLY CHURCH fathers, detailed in writing that Jesus' birth took place on the outskirts of town in a natural cave which was used as a stable for livestock.

So it was, that while they were there,
the days were completed for her to be delivered.
And she brought forth her firstborn Son,
and wrapped Him in swaddling cloths,
and laid Him in a manger,
because there was no room for them in the inn.[1]

Not an ideal place for a baby to be born. There were no freshly painted walls with cute paintings of clouds and baby animals. There was no neat, clean baby bed with fresh clean blankets. It was a place filled with animals, animal refuse, and stench; there were flies and other insects. In fact, everything in the manger would be out of place in any nursery.

We "sanitize" it in the crèche displays on our mantles and the manger scenes at churches. The babe in the manger is representative of God sending His only Son into a world of filth, sin, sickness, disease, and hate. God is holy and pure, but He loved us enough to send His own Son to lift us up out of the filth of our world.

Finding a baby lying in a dirty, stinky feeding trough was a sign, given by the angels to the shepherds; it was a sign of the miracle-working power of God. God has come into our dirty, stinky world to redeem and rescue us, to remind us of where we are, what we are being rescued from... and what the real cost to rescue us is.

Jesus, the Christ, entered the world in utmost humility. A little over thirty years later He performed the greatest act of humility in the history of mankind. An act of humility that resulted in our deliverance from darkness, a darkness we were, and in many cases still are, completely unaware of.

That alone should be cause for celebration at Christmastime.

A Christmas Proclamation!

"Our God is the God of the unexpected.
And few things could be more unexpected
then to have the King of Heaven born in a stable."

~ Bill Crowder

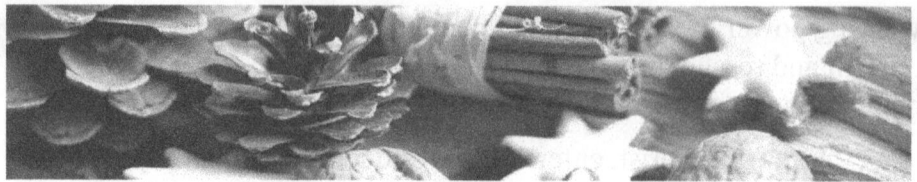

DESSERT

Creamy Chocolate Pie

INGREDIENTS

1 cup milk   ¼ cup nuts, chopped
1 tub whipped topping   1 - 8" pie shell
1 – 4 ½ oz. pkg. chocolate pudding, instant

PREPARATION

1. Prepare one 4½ oz..package of instant chocolate pudding as directed on package, but using only 1 cup of milk.

2. Blend in 1½ cups thawed whipped topping and ¼ cup of chopped nuts.

3. Spoon into a cool, baked 8" pie shell.

4. Garnish with ½ cup whipped topping.

5. Sprinkle with additional nuts, if desired.

6. Chill at least one hour.

Willing Vessels

December 9

WHEN THE ANGEL GABRIEL came to Mary's house and foretold the events that were about to take place in her life, she asked, *How shall this be, seeing I know not a man?*[1]

There are a couple of things to notice in Mary's question. She was not mocking what Gabriel was telling her. She was not saying, "Oh brother! What spaceship did you just land in?" Mary was asking an open and honest question. How can a child be conceived and born outside the natural process of things? And, she got an open and honest response from Gabriel.

*The Holy Ghost shall come upon you,
and the power of the Highest shall overshadow you...
for with God nothing shall be impossible.*[2]

God's prophetic word concerning the virgin birth of Jesus was given and written down centuries before it ever happened:

*Therefore the Lord Himself will give you a sign:
Behold, the virgin shall conceive and bear a Son...*[3]

And it all happened just as He said it would. (Remember – God dwells in eternity where there are no time boundaries. He sees the *end from the beginning*[4], and it was His delight to let us peek ahead of time at the "gifts" He had already prepared for us.)

Mary became the vessel that allowed God to perform the miracle of the incarnation: God embodied in human flesh. Thus, Jesus is both fully God and fully man. After Gabriel finished delivering his message, Mary's response was,

Be it unto me according to your word.[5]

All God needs is a willing vessel who believes what He says is true, even if it is not fully understood. Mary was such a vessel:

And the Word (which Mary believed)
*became flesh and dwelt among us,
and we beheld His glory,
the glory as of the only begotten of the Father...*[6]

Unlike the rest of us, Jesus was not born with a sin nature. It appears that the "sin nature" of man is passed down through the father. Jesus' Father was God, so He was born with no sin nature.

Is the virgin birth worth celebrating at Christmastime? This truth, the miracle of the virgin birth, which allowed God to be made incarnate as a perfect man, is what allowed Jesus to become the sacrificial Lamb on the Cross some 30 years later.

*My soul magnifies the Lord,
and my spirit rejoices in God my Saviour!*[7]

~ *A Christmas Proclamation!* ~

*"The giving of gifts is not something man invented.
God started the giving spree
when he gave a gift beyond words,
the unspeakable gift of His Son."*

~ *Robert Flatt*

DESSERT

French Hot Chocolate

INGREDIENTS

½ cup water   2/3 cup sugar
½ tsp. salt   ½ cup heavy cream
2½ squares chocolate, unsweetened

PREPARATION

1. Heat chocolate and water over low heat, stirring until chocolate melts.

2. Add sugar and salt; bring to boiling, reduce heat and simmer 4 minutes

3. Cool to room temperature.

4. Fold in whipped cream.

5. To serve: place one heaping tablespoon of chocolate "batter" in each cup, fill with hot milk and stir.
Makes 8-10 teacup servings.

Heavenly Dynamos

December 10

  ON A STAR-LIT NIGHT IN BETHLEHEM, over two thousand years ago, the birth of the Savior of all mankind took place. However, prior to the birth of Christ, at the birth of Christ, and after the birth of Christ, many, many angels were hard at work.

  The angel Gabriel appeared to Zacharias, the father of John the Baptist, to foretell the birth of a son to him and his wife Elizabeth.[1] This is important because John the Baptist was the messenger prophesied to come beforehand and challenge people to prepare for the arrival of the Messiah.

> *Behold, I send My messenger,*
> *and he will prepare the way before Me...*[2]

> *The voice of one crying in the wilderness:*
> *'Prepare the way of the LORD;*
> *make straight in the desert a highway for our God'.*[3]

  Preparations for the arrival of the Messiah on earth were now officially underway. It was Gabriel again, who appeared to Mary to tell her she would have the honor of bearing and giving birth to Jesus.[4] At one point, while Mary and Elizabeth were spending time together, they both began to give prophetic praise to the Lord, foretelling the ministries each of their sons would be involved in.[5]

  Now events were taking place that were getting people's attention, *...all these sayings were discussed throughout all the hill country of Judea.*[6]

  Prior to the wedding of Mary and Joseph, when it became known that Mary was pregnant, it was an angel that reassured Joseph,

> *...that which is conceived in her is of the Holy Spirit.*
> *And she will bring forth a Son,*
> *and you shall call His name Jesus,*
> *for He will save His people from their sins.*[7]

It is interesting to note that as a result of this angelic visit, Joseph went immediately and wed Mary. Keep in mind, all of these events were prophecy in action, history told in advance:

> *So all this was done that it might be fulfilled*
> *which was spoken by the Lord through the prophet, saying:*
> *'Behold, the virgin shall be with child,*
> *and bear a Son, and they shall call His name Immanuel,"*
> *which is translated, "God with us'.*[8]

On the night of Jesus' birth, it was an angel of the Lord who appeared before the shepherds with the glory of the Lord shining around him, announcing,

> *Good tidings of great joy which will be to all people.*
> *For there is born to you this day in the city of David*
> *a Savior, who is Christ the Lord!*[9]

The next thing you know, there were angels all over the place,

> *...praising God and saying: 'Glory to God in the highest,*
> *and on earth peace, goodwill toward men!* [10]

The birth of Jesus Christ on earth was an event planned in the throne room of heaven from before the beginning of time. All of heaven was called into action for this particular event. Everything was going to happen according to plan, nothing was going to interfere. Angels were working overtime.

A few years later Herod determined he would tolerate no rivals to his throne. He ordered the slaughter of all the baby boys in the Bethlehem area who were two years old and younger. At that time, it was an angel who awoke Joseph in the night and warned him to take

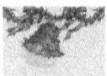

his family to Egypt to escape the bloodshed. [11] After Herod died, it was again an angel who appeared to Joseph to tell him it was safe to return home. [12]

None of these angels were ever worshipped by those they visited. And angels should never be worshipped; that honor is reserved solely for God. But, consider this,

Are [angels] not all ministering spirits
sent forth to minister for those who will inherit salvation?
Therefore we must give the more earnest heed
to the things we have heard,
lest we drift away. [13]

Angels are real. Angels were very busy at the birth of Jesus. Angels are still busy today, ministering to those of us *who inherit salvation*.[14] Primarily to ensure that we *give more earnest heed to the things we have heard*[15], and not let the Christ slip away from *Christ*mas.

~ *Merry Christmas!* ~

"Christmas is a bridge.
We need bridges as the river of time flows past.
Today's Christmas should mean
creating happy hours for tomorrow,
and reliving those of yesterday."

~ Gladys Bagg Taber

DESERT

Fudge Pie

INGREDIENTS

1 cup sugar	¼ lb. butter
1 tsp. vanilla	1/3 cup flour
2 egg yolks	2 chocolate squares
2 egg whites, folded in	Salt

PREPARATION

1. Mix and bake in a greased pie tin, moderate oven (about 350°F.)

2. Serve with ice cream (best), or whipped topping.

On Giving Gifts, part 1
December 11

EVERYBODY HAS ONE. "THE BEST GIFT STORY". It was the gift received, for which you expressed no desire, nor even a hint of desire. It is the gift received, that you had no idea you even wanted. The perfect gift is the one we keep for years and years until it just wears out. Even then, we may gently preserve it somehow, not for remembering the gift so much, but for the memory of the one who gave us the gift. The Best Gift not only touches our heart, but it also makes a home in our heart.

Everybody has one. "The Worst Gift Story". It is the gift that comes... and then goes. Graciously received, (if we are ourselves gracious), yet shortly remembered. It is the gift given out of obligation, not out of consideration or compassion. The Worst Gift makes neither home nor warm spot in our heart. If we are not careful, it may make a bitter spot in our heart. Some worst gift examples:[1]

> Used red suede cowboy boots, complete with dust.
> A manicure set for a ten-year-old boy.
> A re-gifted sweater...worn and stained.
> A wooden pop-out play set for 2-4 year-olds… for a 14-year-old.

What's the difference between the Best Gift and the Worst Gift? The difference is not money. The Best Gift results in something that lasts far longer than any money given or received as a gift. Money is perishable. The Best Gift lasts. Best Gifts are opportunities to show love, care, and thoughtfulness to a person we esteem. Best Gifts send the message that someone really knows you; that they took the time to learn what you enjoy, and made the effort to obtain it. Best Gifts require four efforts on the part of the gift-giver:

Mindfulness
An awareness of the person's character and lifestyle, a knowing that comes through experience.

Time:
Mindfulness occurs over time, it grows out of relationships and produces something that lasts.

Understanding
Looking beyond our own perceptions; looking closely and listening carefully.

Affinity
Basically, this is an appreciation and warmth for the person, looking to the best interests of that person; discerning the difference between their needs and wants.

    Practicality can be given any time. Extraordinary - outside the ordinary - is for a special occasion. Having a dozen presents under the tree is one thing. Having one present under the tree that conveys mindfulness, time, understanding, and an affinity – love – is entirely another thing.

    Don't give too much credence to Worst Gifts. They don't mean you are unloved. They usually mean the gift-giver lost sight of what is really involved in Christmas, and was worn down by all the conundrum of the season. Or, the giver needs a little assistance in learning the art of gift-giving.

    You can help. Instead of writing down a list of things you want for Christmas, make a list of several things you enjoy doing. Then ask for gifts relevant to those things. This way you will still be surprised when you open the gift, and the giver will be pleased with their creativity. When you receive the gift, be generous in praise and slow in criticism.

When you give your gifts, don't use the gift card to say "To" and "From". Use it to say how you noticed what they do and what they enjoy; express love and appreciation. The joy you receive by becoming a great gift-giver far outweighs any bad gift you receive. And *JOY!* is one of the things Christmas is all about. Jesus was right,

It is more blessed to give than to receive.[2]

~ *A Christmas Proclamation!* ~

*"He who has not Christmas in his heart,
will never find it under a tree."*

~ Roy L. Smith

DESSERT

Honey Walnut Gingerbread

INGREDIENTS

- 2¼ cups flour
- 1 tsp. soda
- ½ tsp. ginger
- ¼ tsp. cinnamon
- ¼ cup molasses, light
- ¾ cup walnuts, chopped
- 2 Tbs. sugar, for sprinkling
- 1/3 cup sugar
- 1 tsp. salt
- ¼ tsp. allspice
- ¾ cup honey
- ½ cup shortening
- 1 egg, large
- 2/3 cup hot water

GINOSKO HOUSE CHRISTMAS

PREPARATION

1. Sift flour with sugar, soda, salt, spices in a bowl.

2. Add honey, molasses, shortening, and egg.

3. Beat with low mixer until moistened, then at medium 3 minutes, scraping bowl.

4. Stir in hot water by hand, then ½ cup of walnuts.

5. Turn into greased, floured 9" square pan.

6. Sprinkle with ¼ cup walnuts and 2 Tbs. sugar.

7. Bake at 325°F for 45 minutes.

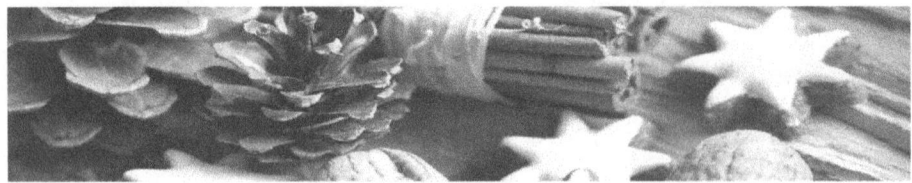

DESSERT

Molasses Crinkles

INGREDIENTS

1 cup brown sugar, packed
¾ cup soft shortening
¼ cup molasses
2¼ cup flour, sifted
2 tsp. soda
¼ tsp. salt
½ tsp. cloves
1 tsp. cinnamon
1 tsp. ginger

GINOSKO HOUSE CHRISTMAS

PREPARATION

1. Sift flour, soda, salt, cloves, cinnamon, and ginger together.

2. Add shortening, brown sugar, egg, and molasses,
and beat into batter.

3. Make as many as you desire,
and keep batter several days in a refrigerator.

4. Roll into balls the size of a walnut; dip each in sugar.

5. Place sugar-side up,
3 inches apart on greased cookie sheet.

6. Sprinkle each cookie with just 2-3 drops of water
to produce a cracked surface.

7. Bake 10 to 12 minutes in a quick, moderate oven, about 375°F,
until set, but not hard.
Makes 4 dozen 2½ inch cookies.

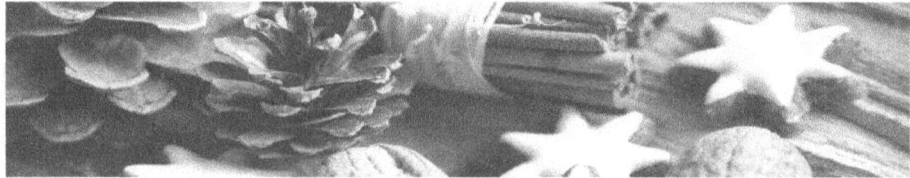

On Giving Gifts, part 2

December 12

NO GIFT WE GIVE AT CHRISTMASTIME, or any other time, will be truly perfect. Time has a way of eroding the value of a gift. There has been but one "Perfect Gift" ever given, and it will always stand the test of time.

Yesterday we talked about the forethought we should make in gift-giving. So, taking into consideration that *"God so loved...He gave..."*[1], let's take a look at God's gift-giving.

Mindfulness:

God took the time to look ahead into each of our lives, seeing the decisions we would make, the lives we would affect, what we enjoy and don't enjoy, what we need to learn, and what we need to unlearn. He took into consideration the individual as well as the whole of mankind.

The LORD has been mindful of us; He will bless us...[2]

Time:

He prepared everything before He ever created one thing. Then He spent thousands of years preparing the Perfect Gift; seeing and adjusting for each person, even allowing a way of salvation before the Perfect Gift was given.

...just as He chose us in Him before the foundation of the world, that we should be holy and without blame before Him in love...[3]

Understanding:

God looked beyond our own perceptions of the way things are and determined the difference between our needs and wants.

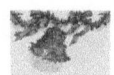

*He was wounded for our transgressions,
He was bruised for our iniquities;
the chastisement for our peace was upon Him,
and by His stripes we are healed.* [4]

Affinity:

He took the time to learn to understand what it was that we were going through, and how to handle it properly.

For we do not have a High Priest who cannot sympathize with our weaknesses, but was in all points tempted as we are, yet without sin. [5]

The Perfect Gift lasts for all eternity. It is not perishable. It won't rust, rot, or corrode. It was not paid for with silver or gold or anything that is corruptible. It was paid for with the precious Blood of Christ. And on the gift card is your name with full expressions of love from the Father.

*The LORD has appeared of old to me, saying:
"Yes, I have loved you with an everlasting love;
Therefore with lovingkindness I have drawn you.* [6]

~ Oh, Merry, Merry Christmas! ~

*"Christmas began in the heart of God.
It is only complete when it reaches the heart of man."*

~ Anonymous

DESSERT

Old Fashioned Ice Cream

INGREDIENTS

2½ cups sugar, granulated

2 Tbs. vanilla (or 4 tsp)

2 Tbs. lemon juice

1 pint heavy cream

4 eggs, beaten (separate whites if desired)

5¼ cups whole milk
(because of homogenized milk,
amount of cream may be cut slightly)

4 Tbs. cornstarch, leveled (optional, but makes it smoother)

GINOSKO HOUSE CHRISTMAS

PREPARATION

1. Dissolve cornstarch in ¼ cup of cold milk; add the 5 cups of milk and cook until slightly thickened; add sugar. Cool.

2. Add cream, beaten eggs, and flavoring.

3. Pour frozen into freezer can and add enough milk to bring up to 3 inches below top; freeze until firm.

4. May be made in hand freezer or electric.

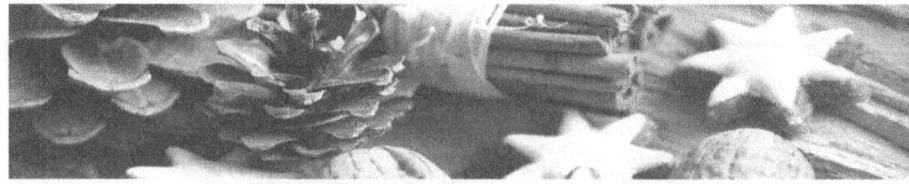

What the Shepherds Saw & Heard... and Did!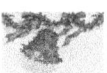
December 13

"Shepherds why this jubilee,
Why your joyous strains prolong?
What the gladsome tidings be,
Which inspire your heavenly song?
Gloria In Excelsis Deo!"

WHAT AN EXPERIENCE it must have been. A warm campfire at night, some of your co-workers nodding off to sleep after a filling meal, and the flock of sheep all settled down for the night. All of a sudden two things happen. You and your friends are greeted by an angel, and the visible glory of God surrounds you! It had to be startling!

Then, the angel begins to talk... to you! No sooner does he make his proclamation:

Behold, I bring you good tidings of great joy
which will be to all people.
For there is born to you this day in the city of David a Savior,
who is Christ the Lord.
And this will be the sign to you:
you will find a Babe wrapped in swaddling cloths,
lying in a manger. [1]

...then there are angels everywhere! The shepherds are surrounded by angels. All the angels are proclaiming,

Glory to God in the highest,
and on earth peace,
goodwill toward men! [2]

    Yes, what a glorious and awe-inspiring experience it must have been. But, the response of the shepherds to all of this was even more awe-inspiring. The angel appeared and said we have good tidings of great joy for *"all people"*, and we're telling you first. So, what did the shepherds do? The shepherds believed what they heard.

Faith comes by hearing, and hearing by the Word of God.[3]

The shepherds certainly heard the Word of God from some pretty impressive messengers. That is the first part of faith, they simply believed what God said was true. How do we know they believed what God said? Because they got up and went looking for the manger and the baby. That is the second part of faith, acting on the Word.

    It is interesting to note that the shepherds were given an opportunity, not a command. They were not commanded to go and look, they were merely told they could go and look. The shepherds clearly demonstrated the two parts of faith:

        1. believing what God says is true,
        2. and then acting on it.

    Faith involves two elements, hearing and doing. Both hearing and doing have to be in operation for faith to be at work. If there is just one part, but not the other, then there is no faith. The shepherds had faith. They heard the Word of God and acted on it. Who knows, maybe they left a few shepherds behind to protect the sheep while the rest went looking for the stable. Then, those who found the stable returned with the report that what they had heard was true! So, the second group of shepherds went to see while the first group stayed with the sheep. Or, maybe they all went at once. Forget the sheep! We gotta see this!

    However they handled it, they acted on the word that they heard. They didn't give it some thought, ask the advice of others, or check it out online. They got up and went.

Faith - hearing and doing - generates another action. The shepherds talked about what they had heard and seen.

*They made widely known the saying
which was told them concerning this Child.*[4]

Yes, the response of the shepherds was truly awe-inspiring. They took in the experience, and it changed them. They returned to their sheepfold glorifying and praising God, and telling everyone they met along the way.

So... has Christmas changed you? What word have you heard this Christmas? The child has already been born. The Saviour has already died, paying the price for your sins. The "Gift" has been offered. Just as the shepherds were given the opportunity to go and see what the angels told them, you also have been given the opportunity to receive the Gift.

Have you accepted it? If you have, how are you acting on it? Are you putting action to the Word? Or, is the Word just sitting on a shelf somewhere in your life? What kind of gift do you think God might like at Christmastime? What is the gift He paid the supreme price for? It is you. What will you give to the Lord this Christmas? Your life? Your time? A real relationship with the Living God?

~ *A Christmas Proclamation!* ~

*"Christmas is the time for comfort,
for good food and warmth,
for the touch of a friendly hand,
and for a talk beside the fire;
it is the time for home."*

~ Edith Sitwell

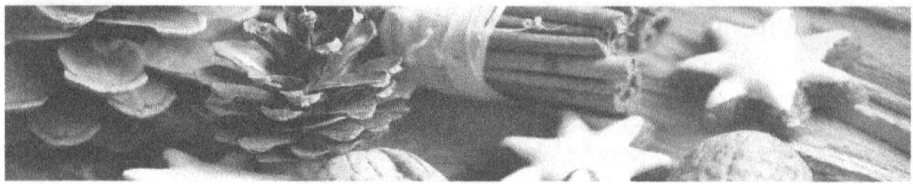

DESERT

Popcorn Balls

INGREDIENTS

7 qts. popcorn, popped
1 cup corn syrup, light
¼ tsp. salt
1 cup sugar
¼ cup water
3 Tbs. butter
1 tsp. vanilla extract

PREPARATION

1. Place popcorn in a large baking pan or roaster; keep warm in 200°F oven.

2. In a heavy saucepan, combine the sugar, corn syrup, water, and salt. Cook over medium heat until a candy thermometer reads 235°F (soft-ball stage).

3. Remove from heat and add the butter, vanilla (food coloring if desired); stir until the butter is melted. Immediately pour over the popcorn and stir until evenly coated.

4. As soon as the mixture is cool enough to handle, quickly shape into 3-inch balls, dipping hands in cold water to prevent sticking.

Yield: 20 servings.

DESSERT

Rolling Pin Cookies

INGREDIENTS	
Cookie Dough:	*Frosting:*
½ lb. butter	¼ cup soft butter
2 cups flour	1 cup powdered sugar
6 Tbs. cream	1 ¼ tsp. almond flavoring

PREPARATION

Frosting:
1. Mix ingredients into a smooth paste.

Cookies:
1. Mix ingredients and roll out fairly thin on a sugared board (use lots of sugar).
2. Cut into 1-inch squares, or use a really small cookie cutter.
3. Bake on a cookie sheet at 350°F for 7 minutes or less. Loosen at once and put on waxed paper.
4. Put two pieces together with frosting.

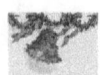

The Beginning of Wisdom, part 1
Master of the "King-Makers"
December 14

WISE MEN FROM THE EAST came to see Jesus, to honor Him and bring Him gifts. Who were they? Where did they come from? What was their purpose in coming? How many were there? Why did they bring gifts of gold, frankincense, and myrrh?

The Magi did not arrive on the night of Jesus birth. They came to Bethlehem long after that spectacular night. Jesus was about two years old when the wise men arrived. We know this because Scripture says they were looking for *"the Young Child"*, and they found Him in his *"house"*, not in the manger.[1]

We also know this because the despot Herod, in his anger after the wise men left without telling him where the Jesus was, ordered all the male children in the area of Bethlehem who were two years old and younger to be murdered.

It is time and tradition that have woven the wise men and their gifts into the story of Christmas Day. Nonetheless...

Who Were The Wise Men?

To begin with, we need to understand that the Christmas story started long before that clear night in Bethlehem. The roots and foundations of Christmas are not found in the Gospels, they are found all the way back in Genesis...

> *I will put enmity between you* (the serpent) *and the woman,*
> *and between your seed and her Seed;*
> *He shall bruise your head,*
> *and you shall bruise His heel.* [2]

This prophetic word, spoken by God to Adam and Eve and the serpent, is the "seed word" out of which all the prophecies for the Messiah, the Saviour, grew. It is this prophetic word which contains the seed for the stories of a virgin giving birth, the manger in Bethlehem, the sacrifice of the Lamb upon the Cross, the resurrection, the King coming to be seated upon the throne of David (which will probably occur sooner than we might think), and other prophecies.

Even in Solomon's time, information about Scripture and God was dispersed worldwide.[3] So, it pays to keep in mind, that during the time the Magi were following a star in the East, the memory of the events of Genesis, the Fall of mankind, the Flood, and other events were still fresh in the minds of men everywhere. However, perhaps the most intriguing aspect of the wise men is that they were influenced by the teachings of Daniel.

Daniel was the young man, a captive Hebrew slave, who had once saved the hide of all the advisors of Nebuchadnezzar. It seems Nebuchadnezzar had a dream one night. To test his advisors, who were supposed to be the authorities on interpreting dreams, he asked them to tell him what the dream was, and what the interpretation of the dream was. Of course, they couldn't do it. So, the king ordered them all put to death, including Daniel and three of his friends (who later became well known for escaping a fiery death).

Daniel and his friends had an intense prayer meeting the night before their execution, during which God revealed to Daniel the dream and its interpretation. After Daniel saved everybody's bacon, Nebuchadnezzar made Daniel a member of this group of advisors. In this role, Daniel exceeded all others in excellence and wisdom. Out of jealousy, the other advisors tried to trick both Daniel and the king into betraying each other. This resulted in the Lion's Den episode. It was after Daniel walked out of the lion's den that he was appointed as head of the king's advisory group. Daniel's title was now Rab-Mag, or Chief of the Magi.[4]

The Magi were a priestly caste which the kings of several successive world empires would come to greatly depend upon. The Magi held dual responsibilities in each of these empires. Those duties included priestly and governmental responsibilities. Our word "magistrate" comes from the word "magi".

Because the Magi held both priestly and political power they became the "kingmakers". As one world empire succeeded another, the magi retained the authority to appoint kings. They were not just authorized to appoint kings, they were *the only ones* authorized to appoint kings! What they said was "gospel" when it came to anointing kings.

This is who the Magi are, and Daniel is now Rab-Mag, the leader of this group of kingmakers.

~ *Merry Christmas!* ~

*"The first wise men gave Christ treasures
from their kingdom.
Today's wise men give Christ
the treasure of their heart."*

~ Holley Gerth

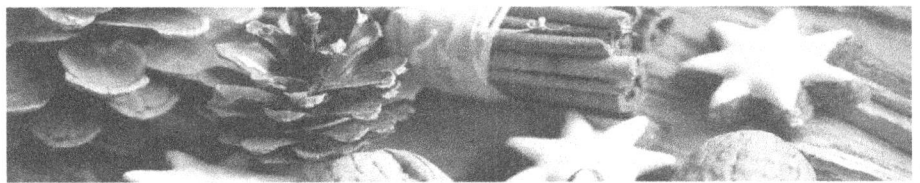

DESSERT

Semi-Sweet Nut Brittle

INGREDIENTS

2 cups sugar   1 tsp. salt
1 tsp. vanilla   ½ cup water
1 cup corn syrup, light   2 Tbs. butter

1 - 6 oz. pkg. semi-sweet chocolate
1½ cups salted nuts, coarsely chopped

PREPARATION

1. Combine sugar, corn syrup, water, and salt in a saucepan; cover and boil for 2 minutes.
2. Uncover and cook without stirring to 300°F, hard crack stage; remove from heat.
3. Quickly stir in chocolate bits, butter, vanilla, and nuts.
4. Spread thinly on greased cookie sheet; let stand until cool.
5. Break into irregular pieces. Makes about 2 lbs.

The Beginning of Wisdom, part 2

December 15

WISE MEN FROM THE EAST CAME TO SEE Jesus, to honor Him and bring Him gifts. Who were they? Where did they come from? What was their purpose? How many were there? Why did they bring gifts of gold, frankincense, and myrrh?

Daniel was suitably prepared by God for taking on his new position as Rab-Mag, chief of the Magi. Daniel and his three pals had been forcibly taken from their own country and homes, marched to a foreign land, and made to live in a hostile environment. Yet, these four boys refused to be conformed to the world system in which they were forced to live. They were good examples of Romans 12:2:

> *...do not be conformed to this world,*
> *but be transformed by the renewing of your mind,*
> *that you may prove what is that good and acceptable*
> *and perfect will of God.*

What was the fruit of their faithfulness? God gave them skill in *"all matters of wisdom and understanding"*, ten times the wisdom, skill, and understanding of their peers.[1] And not just in wisdom, but also the discernment to understand the difference between living by God's Word and living by Babylonian cultural norms.

In addition, God honored Daniel by giving him a prophetic key to end-time events.[2] This prophecy was delivered to Daniel by the archangel, Gabriel, the same Gabriel who showed up at Mary's house. (It seems that Gabriel is responsible for announcements having to do with the Messiah.) The prophetic word Gabriel gave Daniel, known as the "Seventy Weeks of Daniel", would allow for determining the fulfillment of certain prophetic events by counting days.

Being a man of influence and wisdom, Daniel established an "insiders" group within the Magi, a group he could trust with the Scriptures and prophetic visions entrusted to him by God. Daniel taught Scripture and its prophetic emphasis to this group of Magi insiders. He started at the beginning, Genesis 3:15, and brought them right up to the prophetic word given to him by the archangel Gabriel.

By carefully studying Scripture and the prophecy given to Daniel, the Magi would literally be able to count days and determine the time of the birth of the King of kings. The information given by Daniel to this group of insiders was to be carefully protected until the proper time.

It was this group of insiders that showed up at Jesus house two years after His birth. This is how the Wise Men knew the significance of this Child's birth. This is how they knew what the star meant. This is how the Wise Men knew to worship the Child by bringing gifts of gold, frankincense, and myrrh. By the way, it was three gifts, not three Wise Men. A much larger cadre' of Magi showed up at Mary and Joseph's house, and they caused quite a stir in Jerusalem. Wise Men. Wise because they studied the Scriptures.

There are two sources of wisdom. One source is man's wisdom:

> *The wise men are ashamed, they are dismayed and taken.*
> *Behold, they have rejected the word of the LORD;*
> *so what wisdom do they have?*[3]

True wisdom comes from God,

> *The fear of the LORD is the beginning of wisdom...* [4]

Whose wisdom are you using?

~ *A Christmas Proclamation!* ~

*"The early Christians did not rejoice
because of better things to come.
They rejoiced because Christ had come.
God's unspeakable gift was not provisional.
They rejoiced because it was final."*

~ Handel H. Brown

DESSERT

Streusel Coffee Cake

COFFEE CAKE INGREDIENTS

1½ cup flour

¼ cup shortening

¼ tsp. salt

¾ cup sugar

½ cup milk

1 tsp. vanilla

1 egg, well-beaten

3 tsp. baking powder

STREUSEL FILLING INGREDIENTS

½ cup brown sugar, packed

2 Tbs. flour

2 tsp. cinnamon

2 Tbs. melted butter

½ cup chopped nuts

PREPARATION

1. Sift flour once before measuring.
2. Sift flour, baking powder, salt, and sugar together.
3. Cut in shortening until mixture is fine, like cornmeal (rub with fingers).
4. Blend in well-beaten egg mixed with milk.
5. Blend in vanilla, and blend just enough to mix well.
6. Pour ½ the batter into a well-greased, well-floured 6"x 10" (or 8") square pan.
7. Sprinkle with half of the streusel filling.
8. Add remaining batter and sprinkle with remaining streusel filling over the top.
9. Bake 20 to 30 minutes in a quick moderate oven (375°F).

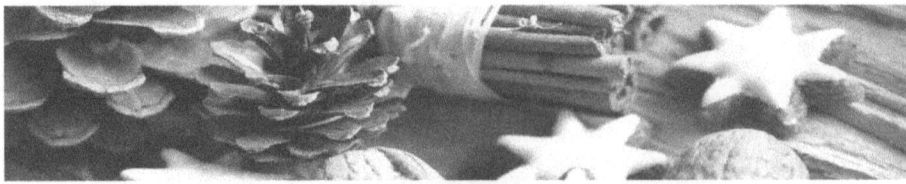

Political Fallout

December 16

AT THE TIME OF JESUS' BIRTH, there were two rival world empires, the Romans and Parthians. The buffer zone between these two empires was Judea. Control over Judea was disputed and fought over between the two rivals. Power and control switched back and forth between Rome and Parthia until about 37 BC. It was around that time that the political power in Rome bestowed upon Herod the title "King of the Jews". It was a title he obviously obtained through the influence of politics and money.

The Jews, however, desired their own independence and were pro-Parthian. Herod had been made ruler over a people who wanted nothing to do with Rome. Both the Roman ruler, Caesar Augustus, and king Phraates IV of Parthia were old and weak. It was time for a regime change in both empires. Herod was trying to hold down the fort in Judea on behalf of Rome, and the Jewish populace was trying to foment an overthrow of Roman dominance with the help of Parthia.

One day, into this hotbed of politics, opposing armies, and dissidents, who of all people should walk into Jerusalem but the Magi! The priestly/governmental caste of king-makers from Parthia! This was not three wise-guys who showed up in Jerusalem trying to cause trouble. This was an entourage. These guys were from the group of insiders within the Magi, the king-makers that Daniel had personally trained in Scripture and prophecy.

Because they were entering the territory of their long-time enemy, Rome, there was a coterie of armed guards to protect them And, these guys didn't bring three little boxes of gold, frankincense, and myrrh; they brought camel-loads of gifts, all fit for a *King*! There were even more armed guards to protect the valuables.

It was a dramatic, eye-catching entrance into Jerusalem, one that could be seen coming from a long way off. People knew they were coming long before they arrived. Surely these Parthian "king-makers" wouldn't have the nerve to enter Roman territory for the purpose of anointing a new king!

When Herod the king heard this, he was troubled,
and all Jerusalem with him.[1]

Herod was right to be troubled. He had gained his title, King of the Jews, through bribes and political chicanery. But here, right here in his city, were legitimate king-makers, the Magi from Parthia. Who were they looking for, what questions were they asking?

Where is He who has been born King of the Jews?
For we have seen His star in the East and have come to worship Him.[2]

It was a question they asked of Herod himself, and it was a political slap-in-the-face. Now Herod knew there was a legitimate rival to the throne upon which he sat. Herod quickly gathered together the Jewish chief priests and scribes trying to determine where the Christ was to be born. They answered Herod with the prophecy found in Micah 5:2, a prophecy which had been given and recorded nearly 500 years earlier:

But you, Bethlehem Ephrathah,
though you are little among the thousands of Judah,
yet out of you shall come forth to Me the One to be Ruler in Israel,
whose goings forth are from of old, from everlasting.[3]

When Herod gave this information to the Magi, he also asked them how long they had been traveling. His purpose in that question was purely selfish. He wanted to know how old the Child they were looking for might be. Then he deviously asked the Magi to come back and tell him where the Child was so he might go and worship too. But God warned the Magi in a dream, and they left without seeing Herod again.

In his fury, Herod committed the barbaric act of having all the male children in the district of Bethlehem, who were two years and younger, murdered. It was a satanic attempt to murder the Christ, the *"Seed of the woman"*, whose arrival was prophesied ages ago.[4] Herod's murderous rage had also been prophesied long ago:

> *Thus says the LORD:*
> *'A voice was heard in Ramah ,*
> *lamentation and bitter weeping,*
> *Rachel weeping for her children,*
> *refusing to be comforted for her children,*
> *because they are no more.*[5]

Had young couples at that time been made aware of these prophecies, or learned for themselves, they would have known not to raise young children in the Bethlehem area.

Jesus came to earth for the purpose of reconciling all men to God, including Herod. But Herod would have none of it. If Herod had bothered to look into the rest of the prophecies concerning the Christ, besides just finding out where He was born, things might have turned out differently for him.

Also, it's strange and sad that the Jewish religious leaders had no idea this was the time for their Christ to be born. Yet a secret cabal of foreign priests and king-makers who traveled from a foreign country knew the exact time. Unfortunately, a similar event occurred at Jesus' triumphal entry into Jerusalem. The Jewish religious leaders failed to accept Jesus as their King, even though they had the *Seventy Weeks* prophecy of Daniel with which to count to the exact day of His triumphal entry into Jerusalem. [6]

Prophecy is God foretelling history in advance. God held the Jewish religious leaders of Jesus' day accountable for knowing the time of His birth, the purpose of His ministry, and particularly, the day Jesus would allow people to recognize Him as King of the Jews.[7]

Even in our day, it is God's desire that we know the times we live in, and what we should do in light of His prophetic word. For every prophecy concerning Christ's first coming there are eight about His Second Coming. What is it we should know about the Second Coming of Christ? Remember, when He comes back the next time,

The government will be upon His shoulder...[8]

~ *A Christmas Proclamation!* ~

*"If there is no joyous way to give a festive gift,
give love away."*

~ Anonymous

ENTRÉE

Baked Stuffed-Flounder

INGREDIENTS

8 flounders (have butcher make good sized packets)

1 lb. fresh crab meat

½ lb. raw shrimp, peeled and diced

1 cup onion, finely chopped

½ cup green onion tops, chopped

½ cup parsley, snipped

¼ tsp. lemon rind, grated

1 lb. mushrooms (or 1 Tbs. mushroom powder)

2 cups seasoned, fine bread crumbs

¼ lb. butter

1 tsp. lemon juice

2 eggs

Salt, red pepper, black pepper to taste.

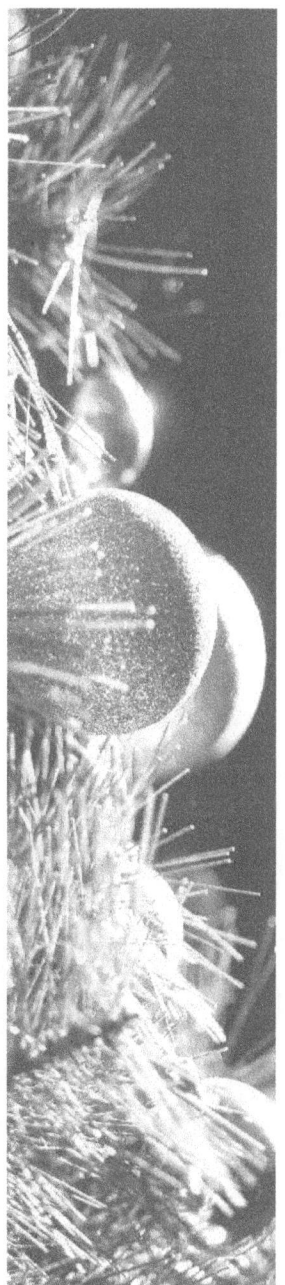

PREPARATION

1. Melt butter and add crabmeat and shrimp; cook over low heat until shrimp are pink.

2. Add vegetables; cook until onions are transparent and wilted.

3. Add lemon juice, lemon rind, and mushrooms; cook about 5 more minutes, then remove from heat.

4. Add bread crumbs, beaten eggs, and seasonings; mix thoroughly, but gently.

5. Rub flounders inside and out with salt and pepper.

6. Fill flounders generously with stuffing.

7. Arrange on a large flat pan (or double layers of heavy foil).

8. Heat oven to 375°F and bake uncovered. Baste often with:
    ¼ lb. butter,
    1 tsp. lemon juice,
    ½ cup dry white wine.

Prophetic Gifts – Gold

December 17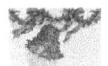

*"O come all ye faithful
Joyful and triumphant!"*

THE FIRST GIFT THE MAGI BROUGHT with which to worship Jesus was gold. Gold is a gift for royalty, a gift for kings. Gabriel had announced to Mary that the Child she would give birth to would one day sit as King on David's throne,

> *... the Lord God will give Him the throne of His father David. And He will reign over the house of Jacob forever, and of His kingdom there will be no end.*[1]

But, how would the Magi know that Jesus was born to be King, and not just any King, but King of kings? We will have to go a little farther back in Scripture. In fact, we'll have to go back to the Book of Beginnings. This Scripture was no doubt taught by Daniel to his group of Magi insiders. Jacob is prophesying over each of his twelve sons. When he gets to Judah he says,

> *The scepter shall not depart from Judah, nor a lawgiver from between his feet, until Shiloh comes; and to Him shall be the obedience of the people.*[2]

Both Jewish and Christian Bible scholars acknowledge this verse as being a prophetic reference to the Messiah. The "scepter" is the symbol of the identity of the tribe of Judah. The scepter also represents the authority of Judah to enforce the Mosaic Laws, which includes the right to administer capital punishment. The person in charge is the one who has the right to administer capital punishment. If you have to ask someone else to perform capital punishment, they are the sovereign, not you. The term Shiloh means "to whom it belongs"; it is a messianic term referring directly to the Christ.

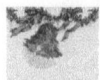

With these points in mind, consider an historic event which gives us insight into the prophetic nature of this verse, and how the Jewish leaders of Jesus day viewed it.

Herod the Great, the baby killer, died around 4 BC. Not only did he kill babies, but he knocked off his own family members who might threaten his rule, including his own son Herod Antipater. At Herod the Great's death, his only heir, Herod Tetrarch, assumed the throne. But he was dethroned and banished around 6 to 7 BC. So, Rome appointed a fellow named Caponius as Procurator and transferred all power to him, including the authority to exercise capital punishment.

At this point, because the right to exercise capital punishment had been given to Caponius, Jewish priests and leaders recognized that the Scepter had departed from Judah. The scepter and the authority to exercise capital punishment had been removed from them and placed in the hands of the Romans. The Jewish leadership had to get permission from Roman authorities to perform capital punishment. (Which is exactly what they did in Jesus' case.)

It is the response of the Jewish leaders to this situation that reveals to us the Messianic emphasis and meaning they placed on the prophetic word Jacob gave to Judah. They thought that the scepter would *never* depart from Judah until the Messiah appeared! They literally thought the Word of God had been broken.

As recorded in the works of Josephus and the Jerusalem Talmud, the priests put on sackcloth and ashes, then they marched around Jerusalem crying out, "Woe unto us for the scepter has departed from Judah and the Messiah has not come." What they failed to realize was this, there was a nine-year-old boy helping out in his Dad's carpentry shop up in Nazareth. They failed to understand the entire prophetic word of God, and they failed to recognize their Messiah.

There were others, however, who did not fail to understand. Old Simeon understood the prophecies and recognized the Messiah when he met Him in the temple. He prophesied over Jesus and Mary.[3]

Eighty-four-year-old Anna, herself a prophetess, understood the prophecies and recognized the Messiah when she met him in the temple.[4]

The Magi understood the prophecies, determined the time of His birth, traveled from the East, and worshipped the Messiah with gifts of gold; a gift befitting the King of kings.

> *"O come let <u>us</u> adore Him,*
> *O come let <u>us</u> adore Him,*
> *O come let <u>us</u> adore Him,*
> *Christ the King!"*

~ *A Christmas Proclamation!* ~

> *"Best of all, Christmas means a spirit of love,*
> *a time when the love of God*
> *and the love of our fellow men*
> *should prevail over all hatred and bitterness,*
> *a time when our thoughts and deeds*
> *and the spirit of our lives*
> *manifest the presence of God."*

~ George F. McDougal

ENTRÉE

Classic Roast Beef
(kind of)

INGREDIENTS

2 lb. Chuck roast

1 Tbs. olive oil

1 lg. onion, diced

1 bay leaf

4 cloves garlic, minced

½ Tbs. thyme, fresh if possible

4-5 cups beef stock, divided

1 lb. potatoes, petite gold, quartered

5 carrots, peeled and roughly chopped

¼ cup brandy
(can use part brandy, part bourbon)

GINOSKO HOUSE CHRISTMAS

PREPARATION

1. Heat olive oil on medium-high heat in a Dutch oven.

2. Salt and pepper roast generously.

3. Brown roast on all sides until crispy, roughly 5 minutes.

4. Remove roast and add onions. Cook onions until soft and opaque.

5. Add garlic and cook for a few minutes more.

6. Add brandy and light with a match, or lighter, to burn off alcohol (be careful).

7. Add Thyme, bay leaf, and stock, only using 1½ parts (14 ozs), of the beef stock. Potatoes and carrots are added later.

8. Cover Dutch oven and place in a 350°F oven for 1 ½ hours.

9. Remove lid and add potatoes, carrots and remaining stock.

10. Let cook for another 1 - 2 hours until roast can pull apart easily with two forks, and veggies are soft.

11. Optionally you can bump the oven temp to 375°F to cook it faster, but watch carefully to not dry out the beef.

Prophetic Gifts – Frankincense

December 18

THERE ARE MANY PROPHECIES in the Old Testament concerning the Messiah, what his ministry would be, and who He is. The prophecies about the ministry of Christ refer to Him as being a servant, a sacrifice, and a king. It was with an understanding of these three aspects of Jesus' ministry, that the Magi brought their gifts, gold, frankincense, and myrrh.

Yesterday we looked at the Magi's gift of gold, a gift for the King of kings. Today we will look at the Magi's gift of frankincense, a gift for a servant.

One of the reasons the Jewish leaders failed to recognize Jesus as the Messiah at His first arrival, was because they were only looking at the prophecies concerning the Messiah as their King. They wanted a king. They were looking for a king to defeat their enemies and deliver them. But, before He could ever be a king, Jesus first had to be a servant and a sacrifice. So, when He was born into the earth Jesus did not come as a king, He came as a servant.

Behold!
My Servant whom I uphold,
My Elect One in whom My soul delights!
I have put My Spirit upon Him;
He will bring forth justice to the Gentiles.[1]

For behold,
I am bringing forth My Servant the Branch.[2]

Jesus exemplified His ministry as a servant by washing the disciple's feet, and telling them, *If I then, your Lord and Teacher, have washed your feet, you also ought to wash one another's feet.*[3] Jesus also hinted strongly at His servanthood when He began His

ministry. One Sabbath He went to the synagogue at Nazareth and stood to read the day's Scripture passage, an ancient Old Testament prophetic text about the Messiah,

The Spirit of the LORD is upon Me,
because He has anointed Me to preach the gospel to the poor;
He has sent Me to heal the brokenhearted,
to proclaim liberty to the captives and recovery of sight to the blind,
to set at liberty those who are oppressed,
to proclaim the acceptable year of the LORD... [4]

But Jesus didn't read the whole passage, he stopped at mid-sentence. He only read the portion of the Messianic prophecy that referred to His servanthood. The rest of that passage refers to His kingship, which will be fulfilled in the near future.

The Magi's gift of frankincense points to Messiah the Servant. Frankincense is collected by cutting the Boswellia tree and collecting the sap. The sap is left to dry for three months until it hardens into a resin or gum. Frankincense was used in priestly duties in temple worship as incense for a sweet fragrance unto the Lord.

Jesus earthly ministry was performed as a priestly worship unto the Father. All Jesus did and said was in complete obedience to God. That's why He could make these statements:

I always do those things that please Him. [5]

He who has seen Me has seen the Father. [6]

Frankincense is known for how freely it burns; it leaves nothing behind. In that sense, it is symbolic of a life of holiness and righteousness, of being sold out to the Lord.

Scripture says we are not to take the name of the Lord in vain. That has little to do with vocabulary, and all to do with how we represent God's name. There are "vanity Christians" today who take God's name only for what it will get them.

Judas was a vanity Christian. He walked daily with Jesus for three years, yet never knew Him. When he stopped getting what he wanted from Jesus, it was easy to betray Him.

Mary was a sold-out Christian. When the time came for Jesus to be the Ultimate Sacrifice, she gave all she had, purchased the costliest perfume money could buy and used it to anoint His feet. Then she washed His feet with her hair.[7]

Jesus was sold out to the Father, and to the will of the Father. He asks nothing less of us.[8] It is a sweet-smelling fragrance to the Lord.

~ *Merry Christmas!* ~

*"There has been only one Christmas —
the rest are anniversaries."*

~ W. J. Cameron

ENTRÉE

Oven Sherried Roast Beef

INGREDIENTS

3 lbs. Stewing beef cut in ½ inch cubes (cutting is optional).

2 cans Cream of mushroom soup, undiluted.

¾ cup dry sherry (cooking sherry is better).

1 pkg. onion soup, dry

PREPARATION

1. Combine ingredients in a large covered roaster or casserole and bake for 3 hours at 325°F.

2. Serve over rice or noodles. Serves 6 to 8.

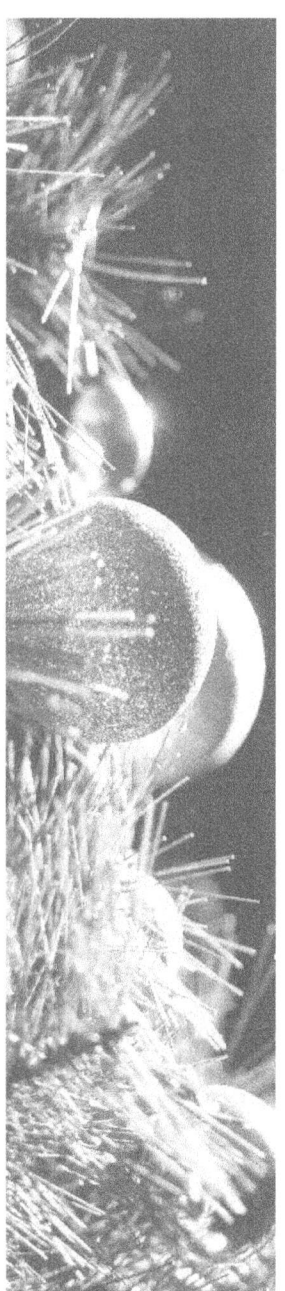

Prophetic Gifts – Myrrh

December 19

*"Myrrh is mine: Its bitter perfume
Breathes a life of gathering gloom.
Sorrowing, sighing, bleeding, dying,
Sealed in a stone-cold tomb."*

THE THIRD GIFT THE MAGI BROUGHT to worship Jesus with was myrrh. Like frankincense, myrrh is obtained by cutting the bark of a small desert tree known as *Commiphora myrrha*, more commonly called the dindin tree. As the sap is allowed to dry it becomes hardened. Myrrh was used as a drug for embalming in ancient times. You would think that an embalming drug would be a strange gift for a small child, but it is the prophetic message within the gift that highlights the importance of this act of worship.

Myrrh was associated with the bitter elements of life. The cuts in the bark of the dindin tree could be said to be emblematic of the stripes Jesus received at the hands of the Roman soldiers. That would contain a prophetic element most of us would be familiar with.

> *He is despised and rejected by men,
> a Man of sorrows and acquainted with grief,
> and we hid, as it were, our faces from Him;
> He was despised, and we did not esteem Him.
> surely He has borne our griefs
> and carried our sorrows;
> yet we esteemed Him stricken,
> smitten by God, and afflicted.* [1]

Rejected, sorrows, grief, shunned, despised, held in low esteem. This one passage of Scripture describes all the bitterness we find in life that Jesus endured. And while He was enduring this bitterness, men thought it was because God had smitten and afflicted

Him for His own sins. In truth, it was because God had smitten and afflicted Jesus, not because of anything He had done wrong, but because of the things we had done wrong,

He was wounded for our transgressions,
He was bruised for our iniquities;
the chastisement for our peace was upon Him,
and by His stripes we are healed. [2]

Another interesting aspect of myrrh is that its fragrance is released only when it is crushed. All the while Jesus was enduring the beatings, the whip lashings, the mocking, the thorns, and the Cross, He was releasing, in the ultimate act of love, a sweet-smelling sacrifice to the Father.

It is intriguing to note that myrrh is also used as a medicine for healing. Christ endured the bitterness and the crushing so that healing could be released to us; spiritually, physically, emotionally, mentally. In every way, Jesus is the Healer.

When Jesus returns to rule the earth as King of kings, gifts will be given to Him; gifts of gold and gifts of frankincense. But, no gifts of myrrh. Why no myrrh?

On the Cross, Jesus cried out, *"Tetelestai!"* After making this pronouncement, Jesus died. *Tetelestai* was a Roman legal term meaning "the debt is paid in full", no further punishment is required. It is translated in the Bible by the phrase, *"It is finished!"* Jesus was proclaiming that His work in paying the penalty for our sins, which was required under God's Law, was done. No further punishment would be required – ever.

Nicodemus came by night and embalmed Jesus body with a hundred-pound mixture of myrrh and aloe. But, three days later the power of God hit that tomb and filled it with light! Christ, the Healer, was raised from the dead never to suffer again. Jesus' death is behind Him. It was done once, for all.

*We have been sanctified through the offering
of the body of Jesus Christ once for all.* [3]

Therefore, no gift of myrrh will be given to the King of kings when He returns to rule and reign on earth.

*"Glorious now behold Him arise,
King and God and Sacrifice.
Alleluia, alleluia!
Sounds through the earth and skies!"*

~ *A Christmas Proclamation!* ~

*"Christmas is based on an exchange of gifts:
the gift of God to man –
the unspeakable gift of His Son Jesus;
and the gift of man to God –
when we present our bodies as a living sacrifice,
and, like the Macedonians (2 Cor. 8:5),
first give ourselves to God.
No one has kept, nor can keep, Christmas,
until he has had a part in this two-way transaction."*

~ Vance Havner

ENTRÉE

Pork Chops Over Rice

INGREDIENTS

4 pork chops	1 cup rice, uncooked
1½ cups water	½ cup onion, chopped
3 tsp. salt	¼ tsp. pepper
2 cups tomatoes, canned	

PREPARATION

1. Brown chops in fat and remove from pan; season with salt.

2. Wash rice and brown in fat, stirring constantly.

3. Add tomatoes, pepper, onion, and seasonings.

4. Lay chops over top and cook at low heat until rice is done.

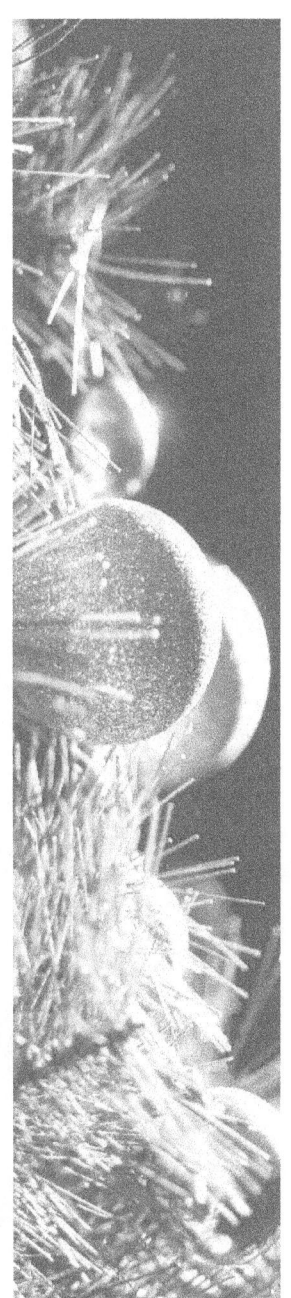

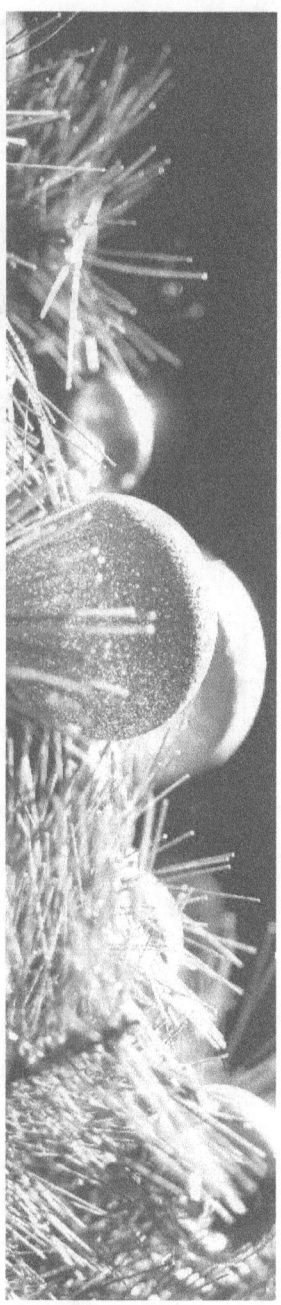

BONUS ENTRÉE!

Pheasant

INGREDIENTS

6 pieces rosemary	¼ tsp. parsley, dry
1 tsp. salt	1½ cup water
Pinch of white pepper	½ onion, medium

2 pheasants, each cut in ten pieces

2 oz. dry wine (white preferred)

1- 4 oz. can button mushrooms
(or stems & pieces)

¼ lb. salt pork or bacon, chopped fine with 1 clove of garlic.

PREPARATION

1. Dredge pheasant in flour and brown in salt pork or bacon fat. Browning gives it a delicious look, so do not over-cook it too long.

2. Add onion, mushrooms, rosemary, salt, parsley, and pepper.

3. Cook 5 minutes, then add wine. Cook 2 to 3 minutes.

4. Cook in a slow oven until tender; about 2 to 2 ½ hours. Serves 6 to 8.

Celebrating Presence… not presents

December 20

THE REAL CHRISTMAS STORY is this: God became a human being in the person of Jesus Christ. The virgin birth, the manger, the angels, Bethlehem, the wise men and their gifts, are all prophetic statements, along with many others, that proclaim the glory of this event.

Stop and think about it. We live in a world of four dimensions, length, width, depth, and time. (Yes, time is a dimension, and, yes, time is changeable under the influence of mass, acceleration, and gravity. It is a fact of physics.) God lives outside of our time domain. God is not someone with lots of time; He dwells completely outside of time. That is why He is able to declare the end from the beginning. This is what we call prophecy, and this is why the Book of Revelation refers to *the Lamb slain from the foundation of the world.*[1] Scripture tells us that Jesus and the ministry He was to have, were prepared before the earth was ever created.

> *He indeed was foreordained*
> *before the foundation of the world,*
> *but was manifest in these last times*
> *for you.*[2]

Scripture tells us who Jesus came to benefit – *you!* At Jesus' birth, eternity entered our time domain and God became a man. It sent ripples of impact backward and forward in time.

> *Behold, the virgin shall be with child,*
> *and shall bring forth a son,*
> *and they shall call his name Emmanuel,*
> *which being interpreted is, God with us.*[3]

That is the real reason to celebrate Christmas. God became a man and lived with us. God came to us to be *"with us"*. That is the reason for the season.

The song is correct. Christmas is the most wonderful time of the year. It is good to be joyous, to decorate our homes in a festive manner, to put out wreaths, and holly, and mistletoe, to have a warm spot in our hearts that reaches out to others. It is good to have a song in our heart and on our lips, to have snow (or not), and good food, and gifts, and family.

But, if this is all done with no thought in mind as to the true miracle of Christmas, then all it becomes is just so much tinsel, and pushing and shoving and standing in shopping lines.

It is when Christmastime is not celebrated with the truth of God becoming a man, that men try to remove Christ from Christmas. They try to shut down manger scenes, and pass laws forbidding the mention of Christ, or forbidding the use of Christian symbols on government property. Yet Jesus paid the penalty of sin for Grinches, as well as for us. Scrooge was correct when he replied to his nephew's Merry Christmas greeting:

> "What's Christmas time to you
> but a time for paying your bills without money;
> a time for finding yourself a year older,
> but not an hour richer;
> a time for balancing your books
> and having every item in 'em
> through a round dozen of months
> presented dead against you?"[4]

But Scrooge was right only in the sense that this is all that matters to those who do not know the true miracle of Christmas. On the other hand, his nephew, Fred, had an understanding of the real reason for Christmas:

GINOSKO HOUSE CHRISTMAS

"I have always thought of Christmas time,
when it has come round
*– apart from the veneration due to its sacred name and origin,
if anything belonging to it can be apart from tha*t –
as a good time;
a kind, forgiving, charitable, pleasant time;
the only time I know of, in the long calendar of the year,
when men and women seem by one consent
to open their shut-up hearts freely,
and to think of people below them
as if they really were fellow passengers to the grave,
and not another race of creatures bound on other journeys.
And therefore, uncle...
I believe it has done me good,
and will do me good; and I say,
'God bless it!'"[5]

Why did Fred think that way? Because God thinks and acts the same way toward us. He left His life in eternity, entered our limited world, and became one of us for *our* salvation.

Christmas isn't about presents. Christmas is about Presence. It is one thing for Jesus to be born in a manger. It is entirely another for Jesus to be born in your heart. So, is His Presence there... in your heart? Is His Presence the wellspring of your Christmas joy?

~ *A Christmas Proclamation!* ~

*"The joy of brightening each other's lives,
bearing each other's burdens,
easing each other's loads
and supplanting empty hearts and lives
with generous gifts,
becomes for us the magic of Christmas."*

~ W. C. Jones

SIDES & SALADS

Grilled Potato Packets

INGREDIENTS

1 potato per person

1 pkg. onion soup mix

1 foil square per serving

butter

PREPARATION

1. Thinly slice each potato into a foil square.

2. Sprinkle with onion soup mix, (a teaspoon or so depending on how much onion and seasoning you like.

3. Place a pat of butter on top.

4. Fold and seal the foil making a packet with the ingredients inside.

5. Grill for about 40 minutes, or until potato is tender. (Or, bake in oven at 375°F)

GINOSKO HOUSE CHRISTMAS

VARIATIONS

A. Bake these packets in your oven at 375°F for about the same amount of time. Test with a fork for doneness.

B. For casserole serving:
1. Thinly slice the potatoes (recommend no more than 6 large potatoes) into a buttered 9" X 13" pan.
2. Sprinkle on a packet of onion soup mix.
3. Divide ¼ cup butter (more if you like) into 8 portions and drop evenly across the top of the potatoes.
4. Cover with foil and bake at 375°F for about an hour or until potatoes are tender.

C. If not eating potatoes, cauliflower works well, but cut down on the cooking time. Cauliflower will bake much faster than potatoes. Test frequently.

Christmas Cheer, It's Contagious!

December 21

THE HOLIDAYS OF CHRISTMAS have been going on for a few weeks now. Hopefully, you've enjoyed some festive celebrations with family and friends. Hopefully, the shopping pressure has not been over-bearing, but rather a time of treasure hunting for those with whom your relationship has warmth.

Every Christmas season we face the same joys and stresses. We know what the challenges are and the preparations involved - decorating, cards, baking, shopping...

A woman was out Christmas shopping with her two children. After many hours of looking at row after row of toys and everything else imaginable; and after hours of hearing both her children asking for everything they saw on those many shelves, she finally made it to the elevator with her two kids.

She was feeling what so many feel during the holiday season time of the year – overwhelming pressure to go to every party, every housewarming, taste all the holiday food and treats, getting that perfect gift for every single person on our shopping list, making sure we don't forget anyone on our card list, and the pressure of making sure we respond to everyone who sent us a card.

Finally the elevator doors opened and there was already a crowd in the car. She pushed her way into the car and dragged her two kids in with her and all the bags of stuff. When the doors closed, she couldn't take it anymore, and she stated, "Whoever started this whole Christmas thing should be found, strung up and shot".

From the back of the car everyone heard a quiet, calm voice respond, 'Don't worry, we already crucified Him'. For the rest of the trip down in the elevator, it was so quiet you could have heard a pin

drop. This year, don't forget to keep 'the One who started this whole Christmas thing'.[1]

That one quiet voice from the back of an elevator helped everyone recover the proper perspective of Christmas.

It is a strange thing at Christmastime. People's hearts really are more tender and open to the things of God. They want to believe in *"peace on earth and good will to all men"*. But people get caught in the trappings of Christmas. They forget the real message and its meaning. They forget His Presence and focus too much on presents. They need someone to light the way for them.

Try this experiment. No matter how hard the look on someone's face out in the crowd, no matter how tired or frustrated people may act, no matter what anger and frustration they are spouting, whenever you get the opportunity - smile. Then give them a warm "Merry Christmas", one that comes from your heart. And watch what happens. All smiles are contagious. One smile is like a pebble thrown into a pond; the ripples keep moving outward. Who knows how far the pebble of your smile will reach?

Because people are more tender-hearted this time of year it is easy to plant seeds of love. It can be as easy as a word of kindness and cheer given with a smile. It can be the quickening of the Holy Spirit in your heart to do an act of kindness for someone, or to give someone a few dollars to help them out. Be sure to pass along the message that it is the Lord Jesus who loves them and who prompted you to act.

You'll see the most amazing transformations take place. Even in the faces of hardest flint, you will detect the slightest softening. Who knows what fruit the long-term effect of your efforts will bring? Perhaps it will generate a conversation with that person that shines the real light of the *peace and goodwill* that is Christmas into their lives. Or perhaps the seed is planted for future nurturing by someone else. Sometimes we plant seeds, sometimes we water seeds. It is God who gives the increase. And God can do amazing things with seeds if we just plant them. Don't hold the Christmas joy inside; let it out in genuine warmth, with the real love of God!

~ *Merry Christmas!* ~

*"Scrooge went to the church,
and walked about the streets,
and watched the people hurrying to and fro,
and patted the children on the head,
and questioned beggars,
and looked down into the kitchens of homes,
and up to the windows,
and found that everything could yield him pleasure.
He never dreamed of any walk,
that anything,
could give him so much pleasure."*

~ Charles Dickens,
A Christmas Carol

SIDES & SALADS

Roasted Brussel Sprouts with Balsamic Reduction

INGREDIENTS

2 lbs. Brussels Sprouts

1 Shallot, minced

2 Tbsp Olive Oil

1 tsp kosher salt

1 cup Balsamic vinegar

¼ cup Honey

½ cup smoked almonds or pecans

Freshly ground black pepper to taste

5 slices of bacon, diced.
Reserve 1Tbsp of bacon fat

GINOSKO HOUSE CHRISTMAS

PREPARATION

1. In a medium saucepan, or skillet, cook the bacon until nice and crisp. Dry the bacon on paper towels and reserve 1Tbsp of bacon fat for the sprouts.

3. While the bacon is cooking, mix the balsamic vinegar and honey together in a small saucepan on high heat. Bring to a boil, then reduce the heat to low and simmer until the mixture has reduced to about 1/3 of a cup – roughly 10 minutes. Set aside to cool.

4. Preheat your oven to 400 degrees (204°C or Gas Mark 6).

5. While the oven is preheating, thoroughly rinse and clean the brussels sprouts. Discard any yellow leaves and trim the ends, then slice the sprout in half.

6. Mix the sliced halves with olive oil, reserved bacon fat and minced shallot.

7. Bake the brussels sprouts in the oven for 30-45 minutes being sure to check and shake the pan every 10 minutes to ensure even cooking. The brussels sprouts should be a dark brown color when done.

8. Lightly drizzle basalmic reduction over brussel sprouts; use sparingly to taste. Top with crushed smoked almonds, or pecans.

It's 'His' Star

December 22

*"Where is He who has been born King of the Jews?
For we have seen <u>His star</u> in the East
and have come to worship Him"*[1]

WISE MEN CAME FROM THE EAST to worship the baby Jesus… well, not really. Yes, Wise Men came from the East, but by the time they got to Jerusalem, Jesus was no longer an infant. Jesus was about two years old when the wise men arrived. We know this because Scripture says they were looking for *"the Young Child."*[2] And because they found Jesus in his *"house"*[3], not in the manger. We also know this because the despot Herod, in his anger after the wise men left without telling him where the Jesus was, ordered all the male children in the area of Bethlehem who were two years old and younger to be murdered.[4] But, what about the Star the Wise men followed?

It is interesting to note this about the Bible: God says what He means, and means what He says. God's Word is pure, and it is to be relied upon. God does not mince words, He does not say things that may lead to speculation, He states things as they really are. God's Word is truth. He expects us to develop the same characteristic with our words. God hates lying.

Men have a tendency to come up with natural explanations for supernatural events. Just take a look at all the "explaining the Bible" programs on TV. Why, did you know that the location of the Red Sea Crossing during the Exodus was only two feet deep?! That is what the "experts" say. That would mean the real miracle was that Pharaoh's entire army drowned in two feet of water! No. The Red Sea was deep. God divided it and made a path for the Israelites to cross through unhindered. It was miraculous. God has that power.

"Experts" have similar types of explanations for the Star. Each year at Christmastime, various theories are repeatedly rolled out about what the Magi's Star really was. Was it a conjunction of two or more stars or planets? Was it a comet? The real explanation is that the Star was a supernatural event brought about by God.

Then God said,
"Let there be lights in the firmament of the heavens
to divide the day from the night; and let them be for signs...[5]

God says what He means, and means what He says. The event of the Wise Men and the star they followed is recorded in Matthew 2:1-12. The Scripture says "star". It does not say they followed a comet. It does not say "stars", so it was only one star, not a conjunction of stars. Nor does it say "planets", so no planets were involved.

The Wise Men were from the East. When they saw the star, they saw it from their position in the East. They probably observed the Star as it traversed the night sky over time, and then finally remained stationary. That is when they began to travel towards the star, towards Jerusalem.

When they arrived in Jerusalem they determined from Herod and the Jewish priests where the birthplace of Jesus was. But, by then the star had moved again. Not over the general area, not over the city, but over the very spot where Jesus was. When the Wise Men saw the star pinpoint the location of *He who is born King of the Jews... they rejoiced with exceedingly great joy!*[6]

These are not natural star-like movements, they are miraculous. Thus, the *"exceedingly great joy"* of the Magi. Scripture does not say whether it was in Bethlehem or Nazareth, but after two years Nazareth would seem more likely.

Something supernatural was taking place. God is a God of wonders.[7] Scripture refers to God as *He who was, who is, and who is to come*[8]; that's past, present, and future. God did wonders, is doing wonders, and will do wonders. The star was clearly created by God as a glorious announcement to mankind of the arrival of their Savior. Both the Star and the Birth of the Lamb of God were miracles!

~ *A Christmas Proclamation!* ~

*"Like God, Christmas is timeless and eternal,
from everlasting to everlasting.
It is something even more
than what happened that night
in starlit little Bethlehem;
it has been behind the stars forever.
There was Christmas in the heart of God
before the world was created."*

~ Roy Rogers

Sides & Salads

Wonder Blend Salad

INGREDIENTS

1 large head of lettuce	¼ tsp. celery salt
1 Tbs. onion, minced	1 Tbs. pimento, minced
1 Tbs. green pepper, minced	2 Tbs sweet pickle juice

3 oz. package Philadelphia Cream Cheese

2 tsp. garlic juice or powder (to taste, optional)

PREPARATION

1. Remove core from lettuce; wash and drain.
2. Blend ingredients into a dressing.
3. Place drained lettuce head into large bowl, core side up.
4. Pour dressing into core opening; cover tightly and cool several hours or overnight.
5. To serve, slice into wedges.

Be Still and Know...

December 23

     WHO IS JESUS...REALLY? Why was He born? What is the proper way to celebrate His birth? Are there pagan roots in the celebration of Christmas? Or, is Christmas a holiday celebrating the prophecies of the Bible being fulfilled? Is the Bible nothing more than old fables? Or do the words contained in it actually come from God? Who were Joseph and Mary? How did they come to arrive in Bethlehem? What is the basis of gift-giving at Christmastime? Who is the real Saint Nick? What are examples of prophecy being fulfilled in the Christmas story? Angels, angels everywhere! What's the big deal?

     We've taken all these questions into consideration. On Christmas Eve and Christmas Day families and friends will gather together. It will be easy to get cozy around a fireplace, or over a meal, or over a cup of hot cocoa. The food will be good, and in generous quantities. Conversations will ebb and flow. It will be easy to interject questions and make comments that will encourage conversation about the meanings behind the festivities, the celebrations, and the gifts. People are more curious than they let on. The events that occurred on the first Christmas were astonishing. Brush up on some of the answers and be prepared to stimulate the conversation.

     Look at it this way, try as men might, the *"Christ"* will never be taken out of Christmas. The "Christ" can be ignored, but the truth is still present under all the secularization and commercialization. The truth is hidden in the symbols, in the religious and cultural images, and in the music. The "Christ" is there because He's always been there, passed down from generation to generation. The "Christ" of Christmas just needs to be brought out into the open. You know:

GINOSKO HOUSE CHRISTMAS

Neither do men light a candle,
and put it under a bushel,
but on a candlestick;
and it gives light to all that are in the house. [1]

  Let the light shine in your house, and in your life. What gift will you give Him this year? Will it be a gift to your family that will last down through the years? Some of the strengths of any family are the memories of the truths that get passed down during Christmas. Strengthen those memories with great fireside chats. Or, as Mrs. Cratchit would say. "Sit down before the fire, my dear, and have a warm 'the Lord bless you'". [2]

~ *Merry Christmas!* ~

"Heap on the wood! - the wind is chill;
but let it whistle as it will,
we'll keep our Christmas merry still."

~ Sir Walter Scott

SIDES & SALADS

Marinated Garden Vegetables

DRESSING INGREDIENTS

Mix the following ingredients in a salad bowl:

1/3 cup salad oil	3 Tbs. Tarragon Wine Vinegar
½ tsp. dry basil	¼ tsp. dry mustard
¼ tsp. ground cummin	¼ tsp. garlic salt

1/8 tsp. pepper

PREPARATION

1. Thinly slice 1 medium red onion and 1 bell pepper.
2. Peel 3 large tomatoes, and cut in small pieces.
3. Thinly slice 2 ½ to 3 cups of zuccini.
4. Turn vegetables over in dressing until well coated.
5. Cover and chill for about 2 hours. Makes 4-6 servings.

For You! Christ is Born! Rejoice!

Christmas Eve

An event that took place 2,000 years ago, is directly related to the problems the world faces today. Jesus had to be born so He could pay the death penalty for our sins:

For unto us a Child is born,
unto us a Son is given...

You will remember when we began these lessons 24 days ago, we started out with this same verse, Isaiah 9:6, and mentioned that it was a two-pronged prophecy. The first prophecy was, *unto us a Child is born*. The eternal God became a human man. He did this with a purpose in mind – becoming the sacrifice in payment of the penalty of our wickedness.

If you're like most of us, we don't think of ourselves as particularly wicked. We are taught from childhood that there is "good" in all of us. Actually – not.[1] We're arrogant. We think we have no sin, or very little sin. We think we are basically good. The truth is, the very roots of our character are grounded in wickedness. The truth is, we are unfamiliar with true goodness, just as we are unfamiliar with God's laws which show us what true goodness is. We needed this Child – desperately! He was born specifically for us.

Behold! The Lamb of God
who takes away the sin of the world![2]

That would be your sin, my sin, and everybody else's sin. Today the "tolerance gospel" is preached, and preached far too often:

God loves everybody (true).

In the end, God will forgive everybody, and everybody gets to go to heaven whether they accept Jesus as Lord, or not. (False).

Men aren't pardoned and free to go to heaven because God is lenient and tolerant of our sinful character. God is righteous, and righteousness demands that the penalty for sin be paid in full. God knew ahead of time, what Adam and Eve would do.[3] God knew the problems all mankind would face because we have a nature that is inherently wicked. God knew the problems we face would be insurmountable, that we would not be able to save ourselves. So, before He ever created anything, God made preparations to save us from a predicament of our own making.[4] God sent His own Son to pay the penalty for our own wickedness. And that is the glorious message of Christmas!

Unto us a Child is born... unto us a Son is given!

A Child who would grow to be a man. A man who would live a sinless life. A man, who even though He never committed a single act of wickedness, would be willing to pay the penalty for our wickedness. And He did just that, dying on the Cross – taking our place and suffering the punishments all of us deserved.

Behold, I bring you good tidings of great joy
which will be to all people.
For there is born to you this day in the city of David,
a Savior,
who is Christ the Lord...
Glory to God in the highest,
and on earth, peace, good will toward all men.[5]

That's the real message of Christmas! God loved the world so much that He gave His Son to pay the penalty for our wickedness.[6] Men are free to go to heaven. Not because God is lenient, but because God made sure that all the penalties for all our wickedness were *"paid in full - tetelestai"*! Only those who accept the sacrifice of Jesus Christ as the "full payment" for their sin will be allowed into heaven.[7]

Make sure you don't miss the real purpose of the Christmas celebration, the real purpose of the birth of Jesus. Do not make the mistake of thinking this event that took place over 2,000 years ago, is unrelated to the problems all mankind currently face.

He was wounded for our transgressions,
He was bruised for our iniquities;
The chastisement for our peace was upon Him,
And by His stripes we are healed.
All we like sheep have gone astray;
We have turned, every one, to his own way;
And the LORD has laid on Him the iniquity of us all.[8]

The "gift of God" is there for the taking. Really, it's the only gift worth receiving at Christmas... or any other time.

For if by the one man's offense
death reigned through the one,
much more those who receive abundance of grace
and of the gift of righteousness
will reign in life through the One, Jesus Christ.
Therefore, as through one man's offense
judgment came to all men, resulting in condemnation,
even so through one Man's righteous act
the free gift came to all men,
resulting in justification of life.[9]

Thanks be to God for His indescribable gift! [10]

~ *A Christmas Proclamation!* ~

*"Christmas is a gift of love
wrapped in human flesh and tied securely
with the strong promises of God.
It is more than words can tell,
for it is a matter for the heart
to receive,
believe
and understand."*

~ Anonymous

Christmas Day!
Tear Into Those Gifts!

It's Christmas morning!
We've waited and waited!

Have you got your gifts?
Have you opened them?

Open them! Open them!
What did you get?

Good stuff I hope!
Cool stuff I hope!

JUST DON'T FORGET all the other gifts. God sent prophet after prophet who foretold the events of Christmas. Remember? He let us peek at the gifts!

God looked after Zelophehad's little girls, protecting their inheritance, placed a blood curse on Jechoniah, yet kept an eye on the proper lineage of His Son Jesus.

During the events of the Christmas story, God's angels were busy everywhere, setting events in order for the arrival of His Son.

God raised up Daniel who taught a caste of king-makers who waited and watched for hundreds of years for the birth of the King of the Jews. He then had those same wise men travel hundreds of miles to worship and bring gifts to the King of kings.

God sent angels to protect Joseph and Mary from the murderous rage of king Herod. And the list of God's efforts goes on. Yet in the end, the Son of God who was sent to show us how much God loves us, died on a Cross. Why would God go to all this trouble?

The answer is easy. He Loves you. But His love is not like the world's love. In the world, our love for someone is dependent on what they do for us, or how they behave, or merely how we feel at the moment. If they treat us the way we want them to treat us, we love them. If they behave in the manner we think they should behave in, we love them. But, if they don't treat us the way we think they should, or if they use behaviors we think are inappropriate, we don't love them. Or, if we just don't feel particularly happy at the moment - meh. We have all experienced that kind of love, so we apply the same attitude toward God.

But with God, love is a character issue. It is in God's character and nature to love us. He created us after all. The Bible states it plainly, *God is Love*.[1] Period. End of report. God loves us because He *is* love, not because we do what's right. His love for us does not depend on our words and actions. He doesn't love us if we do right and hate us if we do wrong. He loves us, whether or not we do right or wrong. And His love for us certainly doesn't depend on whether or not He's having a bad hair day.

God made you. God made you for the precise purpose of showing you how much He loves you. Therefore, you are made for love. You are not made for failure, fear, poverty, illness, death, or any other nasty stuff. You were made to be a recipient of God's love: His success, not failure. His love, not fear. His riches, not poverty. His health, not illness. His life, not death. His joy, not depression. His good things, not bad things.

Most people should be very familiar with John 3:16, *For God so loved the world that He gave His only begotten Son...* What people are not so familiar with is the verse that comes right after this, John 3:17, *God did not send His Son into the world to condemn the world.*

God Is Not Mad At You!

God knows the types of behaviors that will separate you from his Love and from all the God-life He has ready and waiting for you. So, He tells you in His Book what those behaviors are, and what the consequences of those behaviors are: *For the wages of sin is death*[2] - complete separation from God and His love.

God's greatest predicament was finding a way to fulfill His righteousness and to pay the penalty for our sins so He can restore our relationship with Him as recipients of His love. Our greatest problem is our human nature of sin; we can't stop doing wrong behaviors. All of us face a predicament so dire that nothing less than the death of God Himself will save us.

God's character and nature is love. He doesn't want to condemn us, so He put His love into action. He sent Jesus to receive the wages of your sin - death,

> *In this the love of God was manifested toward us,*
> *that God has sent His only begotten Son into the world,*
> *that we might live through Him.*
> *In this is love,*
> *not that we loved God, but that He loved us*
> *and sent His Son to pay the penalty for our sins.*[3]

It is important to understand the last half of Rom 6:23 *For the wages of sin is death,* **but the free gift of God is eternal life in Christ Jesus our Lord!**

That's the true gift of Christmas! God is waiting for you to open His gift. And there are really only two things you need to do to unwrap it:[4]

1) *confess with your mouth the Lord Jesus.*

2) *believe in your heart that God has raised Him from the dead.*

You can pray a prayer as simple as this:

Lord God, it was You who created me, it was You who pursued me relentlessly with all Your Love, and it was You who died on the Cross for me, paying the penalty for all my sins.

Lord, I yield my heart, my soul, and my mind to You and Your Love. I believe with all my heart that God raised Jesus from the dead.

Jesus, I yield to Your Love, bowing my heart before You, and I ask You to be my Lord.

Thank You, Lord. I am a recipient of Your Love right here and right now.

Lord, Your Word says that by Your power, when I receive Jesus as my Lord, I become Your child. Your Word says that in Christ Jesus, I have become a new creation.

Thank You, Father, my old life is over and my new life in Christ Jesus has begun. Amen.

Awesome! Your relationship with God has just been restored. From this point on, there is one primary truth you need to remember:

Nothing can ever again separate you from God's Love!

Yet in all these things we are more than conquerors
through Him who loved us.
For I am persuaded that neither death nor life,
nor angels nor principalities nor powers,
nor things present nor things to come,
nor height nor depth, nor any other created thing,
shall be able to separate us from the love of God
which is in Christ Jesus our Lord.

~ *Merry Christmas!* ~

*"If we could condense all the truths of Christmas
into only three words, these would be the words:
"God with us."
We tend to focus our attention at Christmas
on the infancy of Christ.
The greater truth of the holiday is His deity.
More astonishing than a baby in the manger
is the truth that this promised baby
is the omnipotent Creator of the heavens and the earth!"*

~ John F. MacArthur, Jr.

The Coming King

December 26

OVER THIS CHRISTMAS SEASON, we've considered several prophecies concerning the real reasons we celebrate Christmas. There were over 300 prophecies concerning Jesus' first coming. The prophecies concerning Jesus first arrival on earth were written down long before the actual events ever happened. The very fact that those prophecies were declared and written well in advance of the historical events proves the eternal nature of God. He dwells outside our time domain in the realm of eternity. God declares

*the end from the beginning,
and from ancient times things that are not yet done, saying,
'My counsel shall stand,
and I will do all My pleasure.*[1]

Every one of those 300+ prophecies was fulfilled by Jesus. We can be more sure of the truth and reliability of God's Word than we can of anything else around us.

As we've seen over the last few days, the First Coming of Jesus, which we celebrate at Christmas, was an event carefully orchestrated by God. The celebration of Christmas is all about these prophetic events. But, what about prophetic events that have yet to take place, and will take place in the near future?

Having seen that God watches over His Word to perform it, how sure can we be of the arrival of Jesus the second time, when He returns as King of kings and Lord of lords to rule and reign over all the earth? Are we prepared for His return?

There were wise men who were prepared for His first arrival. But, the kings of the Earth were totally unprepared. They even tried to prevent Jesus from ever being born. As we saw, God did not allow that to happen. The sad thing is, few kings of the Earth have learned the lessons taught by the fulfillment of those 300+ prophecies during Jesus' first arrival. So, they will try one more time, and fail one more time, to prevent His Second Coming:

> *The kings of the earth set themselves,*
> *and the rulers take counsel together,*
> *against the LORD and against His Anointed, saying,*
> *'Let us break their bonds in pieces*
> *and cast away their cords from us.*[2]

Here is God's admonition to those same kings, not to resist The King of kings, but to receive Him willingly:

> *Now therefore, be wise, O kings;*
> *be instructed, you judges of the earth.*
> *Serve the LORD with fear,*
> *and rejoice with trembling.*
> *kiss the Son, lest He be angry,*
> *and you perish in the way,*
> *when His wrath is kindled but a little.*
> *Blessed are all those*
> *who put their trust in Him.*[3]

How about you? Will you be prepared to receive and worship Jesus as *your* Lord, as the King of kings, when He returns to rule and reign in the near future? What follows will tell you a little more about One Who will return to rule and reign on Earth.

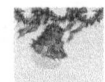

~ *Our Coming King* ~

He is King of the Jews - a racial king;
King of Israel - a national king;
King of all the Ages;
King of Heaven;
King of Glory;
King of Kings...and Lord of Lords.

Do you know Him?
Do you really?

He is a prophet before Moses;
a priest after Melchizedek;
a champion like Joshua;
an offering in place of Isaac;
a king from the line of David;
a wise counselor above Solomon;
a beloved, rejected, and exalted son like Joseph.

And He is yet far more...

The Heavens declare His glory
and the firmament shows His handiwork.
He who is, who was, and who always will be;
the first and the last;
He is the *Alpha* and *Omega,* the *Aleph* and the *Tau,* the A and the Z;
He is the firstfruits of them that slept.
He is the "I AM that I AM", the voice of the Burning Bush!

He is the Captain of the Lord's Host; the conqueror of Jericho.
He is enduringly strong, entirely sincere, eternally steadfast;
He is immortally graceful, imperially powerful, impartially merciful;

GINOSKO HOUSE CHRISTMAS

In Him dwells the fullness of the Godhead bodily,
the very God of very God.
He is our Kinsman-Redeemer and He is our Avenger of Blood;
He is our City of Refuge,
Our Performing High Priest,
Our Personal Prophet,
Our Reigning King.

He is the loftiest idea in Literature;
He's the highest personality in Philosophy;
He's the fundamental doctrine of Theology;
He's the Supreme Problem in "higher criticism"!
He's the Miracle of the Ages;
the superlative of everything good.

We are the beneficiaries of a love letter:
it was written in blood, on a wooden cross
erected in Judea 2,000 years ago.
He was crucified on a cross of wood,
yet He made the hill on which it stood.

By Him were all things made that were made;
without Him was not anything made that was made;
by Him are all things held together!

What held Him to that cross?
It wasn't the nails!
At any time He could have declared, "I'm out of here!"
It was His love for you and me.

He was born of a woman so that we could be born of God;
He humbled Himself so that we could be lifted up;
He became a servant so that we could be made co-heirs;
He suffered rejection so that we could become His friends;

GINOSKO HOUSE CHRISTMAS

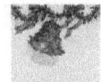

He denied Himself so that we could freely receive all things;
He gave Himself so that He could bless us in every way.

He is available to the tempted and the tried;
He blesses the young;
He cleanses the lepers;
He defends the feeble;
He delivers the captives;
He discharges the debtors;
He forgives the sinners...
He franchises the meek;
He guards the besieged;
He heals the sick;
He provides strength to the weak;
He regards the aged;
He rewards the diligent;
He serves the unfortunate;
He sympathizes and He saves!

His Offices are manifold;
His Reign is righteous;
His Promises are sure;
His Goodness is limitless;
His Light is matchless;
His Grace is sufficient;
His Love never changes;
His Mercy is everlasting;
His Word is enough;
His Yoke is easy and His burden is light!

He's indescribable;
He's incomprehensible;
He's irresistible;
He's invincible!

GINOSKO HOUSE CHRISTMAS

The Pharisees couldn't stand Him
(and learned that they couldn't stop Him);
Pilate couldn't find any fault with Him;
the witnesses couldn't agree against Him;
Herod couldn't kill Him;
death couldn't handle Him;
the grave couldn't hold Him!

He has always been and always will be;
He had no predecessor and will have no successor;
You can't impeach Him and he isn't going to resign!

His name is above every name;
that at the name of Jesus every knee shall bow,
every tongue shall confess that Jesus Christ is Lord!
His is the kingdom, the power, and the glory
- forever, and ever -
Amen! [4]

GINOSKO HOUSE CHRISTMAS

Endnotes

A Note From The Author
1. Jaynes, Sharon, *1 Corinthians 13, A Christmas Version*, <https://duckduckgo.com/?q=If+I+decorate+my+house+perfectly+with+plaid+bows%2C+strands+of+twinkling+lights+and+shiny+balls%2C+but+do+not+show+love+to+my+family%2C+I%E2%80%99m+just+another+decorator.&t=ffab&ia=web>
2. Matt. 4:4

December 1
1. Isaiah 9:6
2. Mic 5:2
3. Luke 2:10-12
4. Genesis 22
5. Gen 22:6-8

December 2
1. Luke 2:8
2. Luke 1:5
3. Luke 1:8-13
4. Luke 1:24-41
5. John 17:3
6. Luke 1:14

References:
Meyers, Robert J. *Celebrations: The Complete Book of American Holidays*. Garden City: Doubleday Books, 1972. Print.
Missler, Chuck. "The History of Christmas: It's Biblical Roots". *eNews*. Koinonia House. 20 Dec. 2011. Web. 3 Oct. 2013. <http://www.khouse.org/6640/BP025/>

December 3
1. History of Christmas, K-House e-News, December 23, 2003
   The History of Christmas: Its Biblical Roots, from the December 20, 2011 eNews
2. <http:www.history.com/topics/christian>

December 4
1. Mic 5:2
2. Isa. 49:6
3. Isa 7:14
4. Luke 1:31-33
5. Eph. 1:4
6. John 15:16
7. 2 Thess. 2:13
8. Isa. 57:15

December 5
1. 2 Sam. 7:13-16
2. Luke 1:32-33
3. Jer. 22:30
4. Isa 46:10

Reference:
Missler, Chuck. *A Christmas Issue: Why a Virgin Birth?*. December 1998 Personal Update News Journal.

December 6
1. Matt. 10:8
2. Matt. 7:11
3. Ps. 68:19
4. John 3:16
5. 2 Cor. 9:15

References:
Copeland, Kenneth. *What About Celebrating Christmas*. His Place 4U
 Web. <http://www.hisplace4u.com/?page_id=915>
Loeffler, John. *Christmas Traditions: The Feast of St. Stephen*,
 Khouse.org. 2000 Web.
<http://www.khouse.org/articles/2000/310/print/>

Missler, Chuck. *Yes Virginia, There is a Santa Claus*. Khouse Enews.
 6 Dec. 2011. Web. 27 Oct. 2013
 <http://www.khouse.org/enews_article/2011/1868/print>

December 7
1. May, Neal W. *Israel: A Biblical Tour of the Holy Land*. Tulsa:
 Albury Publishing, 2000. Print.
2. Genesis 32:30
3. Mic. 5:2

December 8
1. Luke 2:6-17

December 9
1. Luke 1:34
2. Luke 1:35, 37
3. Isa 7:14
4. Isa. 46:9-10
5. Luke 1:38
6. John 1:14
7. Luke 1:46-47

December 10
1. Luke 1;11-23
2. Mal. 3:1
3. Isa. 40:3

4. Luke 1:26-38
5. Luke 1:39-80
6. Luke 1:65
7. Matt 1:20-21
8. Matt. 1:23
9. Luke 2:11
10. Luke 2:14
11. Matt. 2;13-15
12. Matt. 2:19-21
13. Heb. 1:14-2:1
14. Heb. 1:14
15. Heb. 2:1

<u>December 11</u>
1. <http://www.rd.com/funny-stuff/the-best-worst-christmas-gifts-we-ever-got/>
2. Acts 20:35

<u>December 12</u>
1. John 3:16
2. Ps 115:12
3. Eph. 1:4
4. Isa 53:5
5. Heb. 4:15
6. Jer. 31:3

Reference: *The Art of Gift Giving*. The Exponent. 22 Dec. 2011. Web. 7 Dec. 2013. <http://www.the-exponent.com/the-art-of-gift-giving/>

<u>December 13</u>
1. Luke 2:10-12
2. Luke 2:14
3. Rom. 10:17

Reference:
What Can Shepherds Teach Me At Christmas?. Richard Finn. Ezine
   @rticles. 9 Dec. 2013. Web. 16 Dec.
2009. <http://ezinearticles.com/?What-Can-Shepherds-Teach-Me-at-Christmas?&id=3436380>

December 14
1. Matt. 2:8-9, 11
2. Gen. 3:15
3. 1 Kings 4:30-31
4. Dan. 4:9; 5:11

References:
We Three Kings...?. Chuck Missler. Personal Update Nov. 2013. Web.
   30 Nov. 2013.
<http://www.studycenter.com/personal_update/article.php?table=2&code=1150>
Christmas Sermons-Are Churches Preaching An Irrelevant Message?
   Bodie Hodge. 6 Dec. 2013. Web. 10 Dec.
2013. <http://www.answersingenesis.org/articles/2003/12/22/christmas-sermon-relevant>

December 15
1. Dan. 1:20
2. Dan. 9:24-27
3. Jer. 8:9
4. Ps. 111:10

December 16
1. Matt. 2:3
2. Matt 2:2
3. Mic. 5:2

4. Gen. 3:15
5. Jer. 31:15
6. Dan. 9:24-27
7. Luke 19:41-44
8. Isa. 9:6

December 17
1. Luke 1:32-33
2. Gen 49:10
3. Luke 2:25-35
4. Luke 2:36-38

December 18
1. Isa. 42:1
2. Zech. 3:8
3. John 13:14
4. Isa. 61:1
5. John 8:29
6. John 14:9
7. Mark 14:3; John 12:3
8. Luke 14:26-27, 33

December 19
1. Isa 53:3-4
2. Isa. 53:5
3. Heb. 10:10
4. Heb. 10:10

December 20
1. Rev. 13:8
2. 1 Peter 1:20
3. Matt. 1:23
4. Dickens, Charles. *A Christmas Carol*

5. Ibid.

December 21
1. Nelson, Kelleigh. "The 'Christmas Thing' ". *NewsWithViews.com*. 14 Dec. 2012. Web. 16 Dec. 2012.

December 22
1. Matt. 2:2
2. Matt. 2:9
3. Matt. 2:11
4. Matt. 2:16

5. Gen. 1:14
6. Matt. 2:10
7. Job 9:10
8. Rev. 1:4; 11:17; 16:5

December 23
1. Matt. 5:15
2. Dickens, Charles, *A Christmas Carol*

Christmas Eve
1. Rom. 3:10
2. John 1:29
3. 1 Pet. 1:20
4. Gen. 3:15
5. Luke 2: 10-11, 14
6. John 3:16
7. John 14:6
8. Isa. 53:5-6
9. Rom. 5:17-19
10. 2 Cor. 9:15

Christmas Day

1. 1 John 4:8, 16
2. Rom. 6:23
3. 1 John 4:8-10
4. Rom. 10:9-10
5. Rom. 8:37-39

December 26
1. Isa. 46:10
2. Ps 2:2-3
3. Ps. 2:10-12
4. Pastor S. D. Lockridge, Chuck Missler, *The Coming King*.

www.ingramcontent.com/pod-product-compliance
Lightning Source LLC
Chambersburg PA
CBHW081921170426
43200CB00014B/2800